THE MORNING WATCHES
and
THE NIGHT WATCHES

THE MORNING WATCHES
and
THE NIGHT WATCHES

By

John MacDuff

©2012 Bottom of the Hill Publishing

All rights reserved. No part of this book may be used or reproduced in any manner without written permission except for brief quotations for review purposes only.

This book was written in the prevailing style of that period. Language and spelling have been left original in an effort to give the full flavor of this classic work.

Bottom of the Hill Publishing
Memphis, TN
www.BottomoftheHillPublishing.com

ISBN: 978-1-61203-745-5

Content

THE MORNING WATCHES   7

THE NIGHT WATCHES   73

Oct 15, 2022
    I discovered this devotional (originally published in 1853) while reading about my 3rd Great-Grandmother Kitty Winston Carr.
    On Page 13 of "Pioneer Colored Christians" by Harriet Park Miller, Grandmother Kitty asked the author during the interview to read a passage from "The Morning & Night Watches" by J.R. MacDuff. Ms Miller described my 3rd great-grandmother's reaction thusly:
"She clasped her hands &
  looked reverntly upward,
    as if her soul was drinking
      in the spirit of the great
        writer (MacDuff)."
    I wanted to read the devotional for myself, hoping to experience some of the same joy as Grandmother Kitty.
    I was able to order a facsimile of the book from a distributor.
    I read the book from cover to cover & did indeed feel some of the same joy. When I read, "May the

THE MORNING WATCHES

magnet of God's grace continually draw me to Him", I felt it. When I read "Oh LORD, You love me in life
You love me in death
You love me through death
You love me into glory" I felt it.
 This little book makes me feel connected to my 3rd great-grandmother. The eloquent words of JR MacDuff has connected two souls, born over a century apart because we both have a loving relationship with our Father, who is in Heaven.

Evelyn J. Scott

Content

1st Morning
  FOR PARDON OF SIN   11
2nd Morning
  FOR RENEWAL OF HEART   13
3rd Morning
  FOR SANCTIFYING GRACE   15
4th Morning
  FOR SUPPORT IN TEMPTATION   17
5th Morning
  FOR HELP IN TROUBLE   19
6th Morning
  FOR COMFORT IN BEREAVEMENT   21
7th Morning
  FOR LIGHT IN DARKNESS   23
8th Morning
  FOR HOPE IN DISCOURAGEMENT   25
9th Morning
  FOR WISDOM IN PERPLEXITY   27
10th Morning
  FOR STRENGTH IN WEAKNESS   29
11th Morning
  FOR GRATITUDE IN MERCIES   31
12th Morning
  FOR CRUCIFIXION OF SIN   33
13th Morning
  FOR GROWTH IN HOLINESS   35
14th Morning
  FOR VICTORY OVER THE WORLD   37
15th Morning
  FOR DEEPER VIEWS OF SELF   39

16th Morning FOR BRIGHTER VIEWS OF JESUS	41
17th Morning FOR NEARER VIEWS OF HEAVEN	43
18th Morning OR WEANEDNESS FROM THE CREATURE	45
19th Morning FOR LOWLINESS OF MIND	47
20th Morning FOR SIMPLICITY OF FAITH	49
21st Morning FOR CONSISTENCY OF WALK	51
22nd Morning FOR SINGLENESS OF EYE	53
23rd Morning FOR FILIAL NEARNESS	55
24th Morning FOR RESTORATION TO FAVOR	57
25th Morning FOR A PILGRIM SPIRIT	59
26th Morning FOR PREPARATION FOR DEATH	61
27th Morning FOR A JOYFUL RESURRECTION	63
28th Morning FOR THE CONQUEST OF SATAN	65
29th Morning FOR THE OUTPOURING OF THE SPIRIT	67
30th Morning FOR THE UNION OF YOUR PEOPLE	69
31st Morning FOR THE COMING OF YOUR KINGDOM	71

"In the morning, O Lord, You hear my voice; in the morning I lay my requests before You — and wait in expectation." Psalm 5:3

"Let the morning bring me word of Your unfailing love, for I have put my trust in You. Show me the way I should go, for to You I lift up my soul." Psalm 143:8

This little book is designed as a companion to the "Night Watches." It is hoped, by the Divine blessing, they may together form a humble auxiliary in promoting what is pronounced in the best of all manuals of devotion to be "a good thing" — the showing forth of God's "loving-kindness *in the morning,*" and His "faithfulness *every night*" (Psalm 92:2.)

Though more strictly designed for *private* devotion, and therefore expressed in the first person, it is hoped, by the substitution of the plural pronoun, that the following pages may be appropriate for the *family* altar.

1st Morning
FOR PARDON OF SIN

"In the morning, O Lord, You hear my voice; in the morning I lay my requests before You — and wait in expectation." Psalm 5:3

"For Your name's sake, O Lord, pardon my *iniquity* — for it is great." — Psalm 25:11

O God, I bless You that You have permitted me to lie down in sleep, and to awake this morning in safety. You have dispersed the darkness of another night — may no shadow of sin obscure the sunshine of Your favor and love. May the returning light of day be to me the type and emblem of that better radiance with which you visit the souls of Your people, when they are enabled, in Jesus, to behold *a pardoning God seated on a throne of reconciliation and grace.*

I come to You, acknowledging my transgressions in all their heinousness. I have nothing to plead in extenuation. Warnings have been abused, providences slighted, grace resisted, Your Spirit grieved. It is of the Lord's mercies I am not consumed — that You have not long before now consigned me, with all this load of unpardoned guilt, to that place where pardon is unknown.

But I do rejoice to know that "there is forgiveness with You, that You may be feared" — that *I can bring my great sins to a great Savior.* May I be enabled to feel that this all-glorious *name* of a *reconciled God in Christ* is "a strong tower," into which I may "run, and be safe." Give me grace, in self-renouncing lowliness, to disown every other ground of confidence or hope of mercy; and to cast myself, a broken-hearted, humbled penitent, at the feet of Him on whom was laid the burden of all my transgressions. May mine henceforth be the blessedness of those "whose iniquities are forgiven, and whose sins are covered."

May life's joys be sweetened, and life's sorrows sanctified, and life's terminating hour gladdened, with the assurance: "I am at peace with my God." May Your favor brighten every scene, and the sweet sense of Your reconciling love be interfused with all my occupations. If sorrow should cloud or darken, may I be brought to feel that there can be no true sorrow or disquietude to the soul which has found its rest in the finished work of Jesus, and which has attained that blessed peace here, which is the prelude of glory hereafter.

Give me grace to walk more closely with You in the time to come. Being forgiven much — may I love You all the more. May my life be one habitual effort of *self*-crucifixion and *sin*-crucifixion, seeking to consecrate my soul's best energies to Him who is willing to "blot out as a thick cloud" all my transgressions. Overrule the discipline of Your providence for promoting within me this *death of sin*, and this *life of righteousness*. Amid earth's many disquietudes, its crosses and its losses — enable me with joy to look forward to that blessed hour when there shall be no more *sin*, and therefore no more *sorrow* — when every tear shall be wiped from every eye, and when I shall be permitted to know all that is comprehended in the holy beatitude, how "blessed" indeed are "the pure in heart," who are to *"see* God."

Direct, control, suggest, this day — all my designs and thoughts and actions — that every power of my body, and every faculty of my mind, may unite in devotedness to Your sole service and glory. And all I ask is for Jesus' sake. Amen.

"Let the morning bring me word of Your unfailing love, for I have put my trust in You. Show me the way I should go, for to You I lift up my soul."

2nd Morning
FOR RENEWAL OF HEART

"In the morning, O Lord, You hear my voice; in the morning I lay my requests before You — and wait in expectation."

"Create in me a clean heart, O God, and renew a right spirit within me." — Psalm 51:10

Almighty God, who has mercifully preserved me during the unconscious hours of slumber, I desire to dedicate my waking moments and thoughts to You. Pre-occupy my mind with hallowed and heavenly things. May I be enabled throughout this day, by the help of Your Holy Spirit, to exclude all that is *vain* and *frivolous* and *sinful* — and to have my affections centered on You, as my best portion and chief joy. As Your Spirit of old brooded over the face of the waters, may that same blessed Spirit descend in all the plenitude of His heavenly graces, that the gloom of a deeper moral chaos may be dispersed, and that mine may be the beauty and happiness and gladness of a soul that has been transformed "from darkness — to light; and from the power of sin and Satan — unto God."

Forbid, blessed Lord! that I should be resting in anything short of this new creation. May my old nature be crucified; and, as one alive from the dead, may I "walk with Jesus in newness of life." May the new life infused by Your Spirit urge me to higher attainments and more heavenly aspirations. May I be enabled to see the world in its true light — its *pleasures* fading, its *hopes* delusive, its *friendships* perishable. May I be more solemnly and habitually impressed by the surpassing magnitude of "the things not seen." May I give evidence of the reality of a renewal of heart by a more entire and consistent dedication of the life. May my soul become a temple of the Holy Spirit; may "Holiness to the Lord" be its superscription. May I be led to feel that there can be no true joy but what emanates from Yourself, the fountain and fullness of all joy — the God in whom "all my well springs" are.

Whatever maybe the discipline You are employing for this inward heart-transformation, let me be willing to submit to it. Let me lie passive in the arms of Your mercy, saying, "Undertake for me." May it be mine to bear all, and endure all, and rejoice in all

— adoring a Father's *hand*, and trusting a Father's *faithfulness* — *feeling* secure in a Father's tried *love*.

Blessed Jesus! anew would I wash in the opened Fountain. The new heart, like every holy blessing I can ask, is the purchase of that blood which You so freely shed. May it be sprinkled on my guilty conscience. May I ever know what it is to be living on a living Savior, bringing my all-emptiness to His all-fullness; the unworthiness of my infinite demerit — to the worthiness of His all-sufficient, all abounding, grace and mercy.

Shine upon my ways. May I this day get nearer heaven. May I feel at its close that I have done something for God — something to promote the great end for which existence was given me — the glory of Your holy name. Bless all my beloved friends. Unite us together in bonds of holy fellowship here; and at last, in Your presence, may we be permitted to drink together of the streams of everlasting love. And all I ask is for Jesus' sake. Amen.

"Let the morning bring me word of Your unfailing love, for I have put my trust in You. Show me the way I should go, for to You I lift up my soul."

3rd Morning
FOR SANCTIFYING GRACE

"In the morning, O Lord, You hear my voice; in the morning I lay my requests before You — and wait in expectation."

"I am the Lord who sanctifies you." — Exod. 31:13

Most blessed God, You have permitted me in Your great goodness to see the light of another day. May I be enabled to receive every returning morning as a fresh token of Your love — a renewal of my lease of existence — a fresh grant of mercy from the Author of all being. May I seek, this day, and every day, to consecrate the life spared by Your bounty more and more to Your praise.

Lord, I come anew with my burden of sin. It is Your marvelous forbearance that does not make every succeeding morning my last. I bless You that there is still the cleansing blood, the "Wonderful Counselor," the all-gracious Spirit. Give me to know, before I go forth into the world, what it is to have the sense of Your reconciled love. Whether in public or in private, in the communion of life or in the seclusion of solitude, may I realize Your presence. May it be to me the sweetest and most blessed of all thoughts, that a covenant God is "compassing my path" — that by Him I am defended, guided, supported — *safe!*

Heavenly Father, it is the unholiness of my heart which mars the joys of my communion with You. It is my especial prayer that You may impart largely to me of the sanctifying influences of Your grace and Spirit. Let sin be crucified more and more. Let SELF be subjugated more and more. Under the transforming power of new affections, may You become all in all. May it be mine to know, in growing experience, the happiness of true holiness. May I jealously avoid all that is likely to estrange me from You, and zealously cultivate all that is calculated to draw me nearer towards You. "Your favor is life" — O show me that to lose Your favor is death indeed!

This blessed work of inward sanctification is Yours. Alas! I feel my constant proneness to wander from You, and to seek my happiness in that which is perishable. My best resolutions, how frail! — my warmest affections, how languid and lukewarm! — my holiest moments, how distracted with vain thoughts and worldly cares! — my whole life, how stained with sin! But strengthen me with all might, by Your Spirit, in the inner man. My daily cry would be, "More grace! more grace!" There is no sufficiency in myself; but have You not promised to make Your grace sufficient? May I make it my grand ambition to be marking, day by day, my Zionward progress — my growing conformity to the holy character of a holy God.

For this end, overrule all the dispensations of Your providence. May I hear a voice in each of them proclaiming, "Be holy." May I be led to bear them all, and to rejoice in them all, if they thus be the means of bringing me nearer Yourself.

I commend to Your fatherly protection all my beloved friends, and all for whom I ought to pray. "Sanctify them through Your truth." May they all be presented unblameable before You in the day of Christ's appearing.

And may the grace of the Lord Jesus, and the love of God, and the communion and fellowship of the Holy Spirit, be with me now and ever. Amen.

"Let the morning bring me word of Your unfailing love, for I have put my trust in You. Show me the way I should go, for to You I lift up my soul."

4th Morning
FOR SUPPORT IN TEMPTATION

"In the morning, O Lord, You hear my voice; in the morning I lay my requests before You — and wait in expectation."

"Hold me up, and I shall be safe." — Psalm 119:117

Most gracious God, give me grace to begin a new morning with You. Before entering on the world, I invoke Your blessing. Before I hear the voice of earthly friend, or mingle in earthly society, may I have a conscious filial nearness to You, my Father in heaven. O You, who are better, tenderer, dearer, than all on earth, give me the sweet assurance of Your presence and favor. With this, all the day's joys will be joys indeed — with this, the sting will be extracted from the day's sorrows. In quiet confidence I will repose on Your covenant faithfulness. I need no other benediction, Lord, if I have Yours. Other portions may fail me, but I am independent of all, if "You are the strength of my heart and my portion forever."

I adore and bless Your holy name for every past token of your kindness and forbearance. The retrospect of life is a retrospect of love. I am a wonder to myself that You have spared me — that mercy is remembered when nothing but wrath is deserved. "Unless the Lord had been my help, my soul had long before now dwelt in silence."

On that same arm I would desire still to lean. *I am compassed about with a great fight of afflictions, and the sorest and saddest of all are my sins. But I fly to You, helper of the helpless.* Give me to know what it is to dismiss all my own guilty misgivings, and to rest by simple faith on a tried Redeemer. It is mistrust of Him that has been the cause of many a bygone fall. I have been dwelling more on the strength of my temptations than on the strength of my Savior. Oh, "*You* hold me up, blessed Jesus! and I shall be safe." Whenever in the way of sin, give me to realize the all-sufficiency of Your grace. May every hurricane of temptation drive me more under the shelter of the Rock. May the loss of every earthly prop lead me to Yourself — the only abiding refuge. No step in the wilderness journey would I take without You. No loss would I mourn when sustained at Your bidding. No enemy would I fear if You are on my side. *You* hold me up, and then indeed I shall be safe — safe for time — safe for eternity.

And the same support I ask for myself, I beseech You to give to all near and dear to me. May the Lord God be their "sun and shield." May they experience no temptation "above what they are able to bear;" or, with the temptation, grant them grace that they may be able to bear it. And when all earthly dangers and toils and trials are over, may we all be enabled to meet in glory, and trace there, with adoring gratitude and joy, the way in which *Your* mercy through life "has held us up."

Anew I commend myself, body and soul, to You this day. For Your dear Son's sake, forgive all my sins. My sole trust is in the atoning blood. May I feel this to be the best preservative against temptation and sin, that all I am, and all I have, is not my own, but belongs to the Lord who died for me. Hear these my unworthy supplications, and grant me an answer in peace, for His sake. Amen.

"Let the morning bring me word of Your unfailing love, for I have put my trust in You. Show me the way I should go, for to You I lift up my soul."

5th Morning
FOR HELP IN TROUBLE

"In the morning, O Lord, You hear my voice; in the morning I lay my requests before You — and wait in expectation."

"Though I walk in the midst of trouble, You will revive me." — Psalm 138:7

Most blessed Lord, who have again permitted me to approach a throne of grace, shine this day into my heart. Anew may I enter on another day's duties and trials, with a soul calm and peaceful amid all other disquietudes, by being at peace with You.

I bless You that I can ever "sing of mercy" as well as of "judgment." Your dealings might have been all in unmixed wrath, but the severest of them are tempered with gracious love. Oh that they may have their designed effect of driving me to the only true rest for the soul, in the bosom of its God! May the breaking of cistern by cistern only endear to me the more the great Fountain-head.

How often do You send tribulations, that Your people may see more of Your gracious hand! How often, when the waters are troubled, do we recognize the presence of the great Covenant-angel himself, and experience the plenitude of His upholding grace and mercy! Lord, my earnest prayer is, that every trial may serve to unfold to me more of the preciousness of Jesus. As prop by prop, which used to support me on earth, may be giving way, may I know what it is to lean my whole weight *upon* Him, and leave my whole case *with* Him, repairing to Him as the friend that "sticks closer than any brother" — into His sympathizing bosom to confide my every need — from His inexhaustible treasury to draw every consolation — and on His upholding arm confidingly and habitually to rest.

What, O blessed Savior, are my troubles to Yours! What are my bitterest tears and most aching heart in comparison with what You so freely endured for me! May the remembrance of this *Your* fellowship in my suffering, and *my* fellowship in *Yours,* reconcile me patiently to endure whatever You see fit to lay upon me. Give me grace ever to see that my bitterest trial is my sin, that my heaviest cross is the cross of my wandering treacherous heart. When I think of that blessed time when God shall terminate the tears of a weeping world, may this be my loftiest ground of rejoicing — that there will be then no more sin to cause them.

Humbly I would lie at my Savior's feet, disowning all trust except in Him — exulting in His finished work, and meritorious righteousness, and all-prevalent intercession. I rejoice to think of the redeemed multitude before His throne, "whom no man can number," and to feel that His ability and willingness "to save unto the uttermost" are still the same.

Command, O Lord, Your richest blessing this day on all whom I love. May all my relatives be related to You in the common bonds of the gospel. Though separated by distance from each other on life's highway, may we enjoy the consolation that we are all treading the same invisible road Zionward — that earth's dearest and tenderest ties will, at the end of the checkered journey, be strengthened and perpetuated in the full vision and fruition of You our God.

May the grace of the Lord Jesus, and the love of God, and the fellowship and communion of the Holy Spirit, be with me this day and ever. Amen.

"Let the morning bring me word of Your unfailing love, for I have put my trust in You. Show me the way I should go, for to You I lift up my soul."

6th Morning
FOR COMFORT IN BEREAVEMENT

"In the morning, O Lord, You hear my voice; in the morning I lay my requests before You — and wait in expectation." Psalm 5:3

"Turn to me, and have mercy upon me, for I am desolate and afflicted." — Psalm 25:16

"O God, I come to You this morning, rejoicing in the simple but sublime assurance that "the Lord reigns." Your judgments are often "a great deep." May it be mine ever to own Your sovereignty, and to rest satisfied with the assurance, "He has done all things well."

It is indeed my comfort to know that "my times" are not in my own hands, but in Yours. When in vain I seek to explain *the mystery of Your inscrutable doings*, may I be enabled implicitly to trust Your unswerving rectitude and faithfulness. The kindest and best of earthly parents may err — they may be betrayed into unnecessary harshness and severity — but You, O unerring Parent, will not, and cannot inflict one unneeded stroke. I can own Your wisdom where I cannot discern it. I can trust the footsteps of love where I cannot trace them.

I look back with adoring wonder on all Your marvelous dealings towards me in the past. "When my foot slipped, Your mercy, O Lord, held me up." How many tear-drops have been dried by You! How many sorrows have been soothed by you! How many dangers have been averted by you! Instead of wondering at my trials, I have rather reason to marvel at Your forbearance. What are my heaviest afflictions in comparison with the deservings of sin? Lord, if they had been in proportion to my guilt, I could not have had one hour of joy.

Give me grace not only to bear all, and to endure all, but to glory in all which Your chastening love sees fit to appoint. Affliction is your own appointed training-school for immortality. If I need such training, Lord, withhold it not. Rather subject me to the severest ordeal of fatherly discipline, than leave me to vex You more with my guilty departures and backsliding. I will confide in the tenderness of Your dealings — that You will conduct me by no rougher path than is really needful. You have given Your Son for me! After *such* a pledge of Your love, may it never be mine to breathe one murmuring word.

For all in sorrow, Lord, I pray that they may take their sorrows to the "Man of sorrows." May they be willing to forget their own light afflictions as they behold His bleeding wounds. Blessed God, what a source of joy to the whole family of the afflicted, that the exalted Head and elder Brother has Himself tasted sorrow's bitterest cup! Lord Jesus, You who have suffered so much for me, grant that by patience and uncomplaining submission I may be enabled to "glorify you in the fires."

All my beloved friends I commit to Your care. May the Lord be their everlasting portion. Forbid that I should have to mourn in them what would be bitterer than the pang of all earthly bereavement — that they are bereft of Your favor. Make them Yours, and in the midst of life's vicissitudes and changes, may we all look forward to that better time, and that better world, where sorrow and sighing shall forever flee away. And all I ask is for Jesus' sake. Amen.

"Let the morning bring me word of Your unfailing love, for I have put my trust in You. Show me the way I should go, for to You I lift up my soul."

7th Morning
FOR LIGHT IN DARKNESS

"In the morning, O Lord, You hear my voice; in the morning I lay my requests before You — and wait in expectation."
"To the upright there arises light in the darkness." — Psalm 103:4

Eternal, everlasting God, I bless You for the privilege of access into Your presence. What am I — a guilty, unworthy sinner, deserving only of condemnation — that I should be permitted, with holy boldness, to approach the footstool of Your throne and call You "my Father in heaven!"

I rejoice to know, when "my heart is overwhelmed, and in perplexity," that I can ever look to You as a "Rock that is higher than I" — that, amid all the ebbings and flowings in the tide of my own fitful frames and feelings, You, great Rock of ages, remain fixed and immovable. You have never failed me in the past. When "deep has been calling to deep," and many "waves and billows have gone over me," "the Lord has commanded His loving-kindness in the daytime, and in the night His song has been with me, and my prayer to the God of my life." And I will trust You in the future. In the midst of baffling and mysterious providences I will be still — hushing every murmur, and breathing in lowly resignation the prayer, "divinely taught," "Your will be done."

It is my comfort to know that the darkest cloud is fringed with covenant love. I can repose on the blessed assurance that *present* discipline is *needed* discipline, and that all which is mystery now will be cleared up hereafter. May it be mine cheerfully to follow the footsteps of the guiding Shepherd through the darkest, loneliest road, and amid thickening sorrows may I have grace to say, "Though He slays me, yet will I trust in Him."

Lord, increase my faith — let it rise above all difficulties and all trials. Let these drive me closer to Him who has promised to make me "more than conqueror." Let them quicken my longings for the true home of my soul above. May it be my grand ambition here to be a "pilgrim" in everything — to be pitching my tent day by day nearer heaven, imbibing every day more of the pilgrim character, and longing more for the pilgrim's rest. May I be enabled to say, with an increasingly chastened spirit, of a passing world, "Here I have no continuing city." May this assurance dry all tears, and reconcile to all sorrows — "I am journeying to the place of which the Lord has said, I will give it you."

Blessed Jesus, hasten Your coming and Your kingdom. Scatter the darkness which is now covering heathen nations. Stand by Your missionary servants. May they exercise a simple faith on Your own sure word of promise. "Strong in the Lord and in the power of His might," may every mountain of difficulty be made a plain, and "the glory of the Lord be revealed."

God of Bethel, I commend to You all my beloved friends. Shield them by Your protecting providence. Give them every needed blessing in the present life, and in the world to come life everlasting. And all I ask is for Jesus' sake. Amen.

"Let the morning bring me word of Your unfailing love, for I have put my trust in You. Show me the way I should go, for to You I lift up my soul."

8th Morning
FOR HOPE IN DISCOURAGEMENT

"In the morning, O Lord, You hear my voice; in the morning I lay my requests before You — and wait in expectation."

"Why are you downcast, O my soul, and why are you disturbed within me? Hope in God." — Psalm 43:5

O God, in Your infinite mercy You have again spared me to approach Your blessed presence. May each morning find me better prepared for the glorious waking-time of immortality, when "the day shall break," and earth's shadows shall forever "flee away." May I seek to rise this day in newness of life, breathing more of the atmosphere of holiness, and partaking more of the character of heaven.

You are always, by the salutary dispensations of Your providence, reminding me that "earth is not my rest." It is well, Lord, that it should be so; that, by Your own gracious and needed discipline, the world be disarmed of its insinuating power, and I be weaned from what is precarious at the best, and which ultimately *must* perish.

O my God, I feel heavily burdened by reason of sin. I mourn my guilty proneness to temptation. How anything and everything seems often enough to drive me from you, and to lead me to seek my happiness in created good, rather than in Yourself, the infinite fountain of all excellence! How sad have been my backslidings! — how have solemn vows been broken! — how have abandoned and forsworn sins threatened again to have dominion over me! How little tenderness of conscience has there been! — how little dread of an uneven walk! How often, on the heart which I have consecrated to You as an altar for the perpetual sacrifice of praise, and gratitude, and love, has there been burning incense to strange gods!

Lord, when I look to my inner self I have good cause indeed for misgivings and despondency. Conscience repeats, over and over again, a sentence of condemnation, and I have nothing to extenuate my guilt or excuse my sin. Where can I flee? Where can I look but to You, O Lamb of God, sin-bearing and sin-forgiving Savior!

Enable me to be living more from moment to moment on Your grace — to rely on Your guiding arm with more childlike confidence — to look with a more simple faith to Your finished work, disowning all trust in my own doings, and casting myself, as a poor needy pensioner, on the bounty of Him who has done all, and suffered all, and endured all, for me. Thus relying on the unseen arm of a covenant-God, when the hour of darkness and discouragement overtakes me — when trials multiply, and comforts fail, and streams of earthly blessings are dried up — may I have what compensates for the loss of all, "Your favor, which is life, and Your loving-kindness, which is better than life." "I will go in the strength of the Lord God." "Though He slays me, yet will I trust in Him."

Be the God of all near and dear to me. May all my relatives be able to claim a spiritual relationship with You, that so those earthly bonds of attachment, which sooner or later must snap asunder here, may be renewed and perpetuated before the throne.

Pity all who are in sorrow. Comfort the feeble-minded. May "the joy of the Lord be their strength." May valuable lives be prolonged. May those appointed unto death be prepared for their great change. And all I ask is for Jesus' sake. Amen.

"Let the morning bring me word of Your unfailing love, for I have put my trust in You. Show me the way I should go, for to You I lift up my soul."

9th Morning
FOR WISDOM IN PERPLEXITY

"In the morning, O Lord, You hear my voice; in the morning I lay my requests before You — and wait in expectation."
"Cause me to know the way wherein I should walk, for I lift up my soul to You." — Psalm 143:8

O eternal Lord, whose nature and whose name is love, I bless You that I am again invited into Your presence. What am I, that I should be permitted to speak to the infinite God! I might have been left through eternity a monument of Your righteous vengeance. I might have known You only as "the consuming fire." But "Your ways are not as man's ways;" mercy is remembered when wrath might have come upon me to the uttermost.

I desire to begin this day, blessing and praising You for "Your unspeakable gift," Jesus the Son of Your love. Adored be your name, that the guilt of my sin, which the holiness of Your law could not permit otherwise to be cancelled, has to Him been transferred — that, as the scape-goat of His people, He has borne the mighty load into the land of oblivion, never more to be remembered. May I be enabled to show forth my lively gratitude to You for this wondrous token of Your Love, not only by lip homage, but by heart and life devotion. Sanctify and seal me in body, soul and spirit; and present me at last "faultless before the presence of Your glory with exceeding joy."

O my God, I rejoice to know that my interests for time and eternity are confided to Your keeping. Though often "wonderful in counsel," You are ever "excellent in working." You are "God only wise" — "righteous in all Your ways, and holy in all Your works." I commit my way and my doings unto You. "*You* hold me up, and I shall be safe." May I trust Your wisdom and faithfulness even amid crosses and losses, and frowning providences. Make them all work together for my good.

If my path be in any way now hedged up with thorns, "undertake for me," "Guide me with Your counsel." Let me take no step, and engage in no plan, unsanctioned by Your approval. Let it be my grand aim and ambition, in all the changes of a changing life, to hear Your directing voice, saying, "This is the way, walk in it;" and then shall all life's trials be sweetened, and life's burden lightened, by knowing that they are the appointment of infinite wisdom and unchanging love, and that, though man may err, God never can.

May Your Holy Spirit lead me this day into all the truth. May all its duties be pervaded by the leavening power of vital godliness. While in the world, may I seek to feel and to exhibit that I am not of it. May I give evidence, in my walk and conversation, of a renewed nature, and of a nobler destiny.

Hasten, blessed Jesus, Your coming and Your kingdom. "How long shall the wicked triumph?" "Save Your people, and bless Your inheritance; feed them also, and lift them up forever."

Let the voice of salvation be heard in the household of all I love. May theirs be the dwellings of the righteous. May this be their name, "The Lord is there." May they know Him who has said, "I will never leave you nor forsake you."

And "now, Lord, what do I wait for? my hope is in You." Hear and answer these unworthy supplications, for Jesus' sake. Amen.

"Let the morning bring me word of Your unfailing love, for I have put my trust in You. Show me the way I should go, for to You I lift up my soul."

10th Morning
FOR STRENGTH IN WEAKNESS

"In the morning, O Lord, You hear my voice; in the morning I lay my requests before You — and wait in expectation."

"My strength is made perfect in weakness." — 2 Cor. 12:9

O high and mighty God, inhabiting eternity, draw near to a poor unworthy sinner, who ventures anew this morning to approach the footstool of Your throne. Give me now the gracious aids of Your gracious Spirit, that out of much weakness I may be made strong. It is Your own gracious assurance, that "those who wait upon the Lord shall renew their strength." I would rely on the faithfulness of a promising God. May my own utter emptiness drive me to all fullness. May my own conscious weakness wean me from all earthly props, and confidences, and refuges, to "abide under the shadow of the Almighty."

Lord, I confess this day with shame and confusion of face my many infirmities, my coldness and lukewarmness, my distrust of Your providence, my insensibility to Your Love, my murmuring at Your dealings, my tampering with sin, my resisting of Your grace. How often, like the slender reed, have I bent before the blast of temptation, my best resolutions proving "as the morning cloud and the early dew!"

And yet gracious Father, You have not broken "the bruised reed" — You have not "quenched the smoking flax." I am here this morning a marvel to myself that You are still sparing me. "Your ways are not as man's ways." Had it been so, You would long since have grown weary. But it is the prerogative of the everlasting God that "*He* faints not, neither is weary." You are this morning giving me fresh grants of mercy, renewed proofs and tokens of unmerited love. I am receiving "at the Lord's hand double for all my sins."

I rejoice to know, blessed Jesus, it is Your burdened ones You have specially promised "gently to lead." You will conduct me by no rougher road than is necessary. "Undertake for me." May the wilderness journey be this day resumed and renewed with a more simple, and childlike, and habitual leaning on You. Put this new song into my mouth, "The Lord is my Rock, and my fortress, and my deliverer; my God, my strength, in whom I will trust." Say to me, in the midst of my weakness, "Fear not, you worm Jacob." With the pillar of Your presence ever before me, "I will go from strength to strength."

Keep me this day from sin. May no evil thoughts, or vain imaginings, or deceitful lusts, obtrude on my walk with God. May an affecting sense of how frail I am, keep me near the atoning sacrifice. May the "horns of the altar" ever be in sight. Blessed Jesus, my helpless soul would hang, every moment upon You.

Look down in Your kindness on all connected with me by ties of earthly kindred. May the blessing of the God of Bethel rest on every heart and household I love. May we all be journeying Zionwards, and be so weaned from earth as to feel that Zionwards is homewards. If pursuing different paths, and separated, it may be, far from one another, may the journey have one blessed and happy termination. May we meet in glory, and meet with You. And all I ask is for the Redeemer's sake. Amen.

"Let the morning bring me word of Your unfailing love, for I have put my trust in You. Show me the way I should go, for to You I lift up my soul."

11th Morning
FOR GRATITUDE IN MERCIES

"In the morning, O Lord, You hear my voice; in the morning I lay my requests before You — and wait in expectation."
"What shall I render to the Lord for all His benefits towards me?" — Psalm 116:12

O God, I adore You as the Author and Giver of every good and every perfect gift. You are daily loading me with Your benefits. Every returning morning brings with it fresh causes for gratitude — new material for praise. I bless You for Your temporal bounties — "how great has been the sum of them!" While others have been pining in poverty, or wasted by sickness, or racked in pain, or left friendless and portionless, You have been making showers of blessing to fall around my dwelling. I laid me down last night and slept — I awoke, for the Lord sustained me. I might never have seen the morning light. Mine might have been the midnight summons to meet a God in whose righteous presence I was all unfit and unprepared to stand. And yet I am again spared, a monument of Your goodness. Oh, enkindle a flame of undying gratitude to You, on the clay-cold altar of my heart. I mourn and lament that I am so little and so feebly affected by the magnitude of Your mercies, and especially by the riches of Your grace and love manifested in Jesus — that my affections are so little alive to the incalculable obligation under which I am laid to Him who has "loved me with an everlasting love." I am doubly Yours. Creation and redemption combine in claiming all I am, and all I have, for You and Your service. Good Lord, preserve me from the sin of insensibility to Your unwearied kindness — of taking Your mercies as matters of course, and thus living in a state of independence of You. May my whole existence become a sacrifice of praise and thanksgiving — may all my doings testify the sincerity and devotion of a heart feeling alive to every gift of the great Giver; and, especially, may I be so brought under the constraining influence of redeeming love, as to consecrate every power of my body and every faculty of my soul to Him who so willingly consecrated and shed His very life's blood for me.

Lord, this day shine upon me with the light of Your countenance; may every mercy I experience in the course of it be hallowed and sweetened by the thought that it comes from God. And, while ever mindful and thankful in the midst of present mercies, teach me to keep in view the crowning mercy of all — the hope of at last sharing Your presence and full fruition, and of joining in the eternal ascription with the ransomed multitude above, who cease not day nor night to celebrate Your praises.

Bless all near and dear to me. Defend them by Your mighty power. Give *them,* too, gratitude for mercies past, and the sure and well-grounded hope of a glorious inheritance in that better world, where mercy is unmixed with judgment, and joy undarkened by sorrow. And all I ask is for Jesus' sake. Amen.

"Let the morning bring me word of Your unfailing love, for I have put my trust in You. Show me the way I should go, for to You I lift up my soul."

12th Morning
FOR CRUCIFIXION OF SIN

"In the morning, O Lord, You hear my voice; in the morning I lay my requests before You — and wait in expectation."

"I die daily." — 1 Cor. 15:31

Heavenly Father, who have permitted me, in Your great mercy, to see the light of another day, enable me to begin and to end it with You. Let all my thoughts and purposes and actions have the superscription written on them — "Holiness to the Lord."

Give me to know the blessedness of reconciliation — what it is, as a sinner, and the chief of sinners, to come "just as I am, without one plea," to that blood "which cleanses from all sin." I desire to take hold of the sublime assurance that Jesus is "able to save unto the uttermost" — that He has left nothing for me as a suppliant at Your throne — a pensioner on Your bounty — but to accept all as the gift and purchase of free, unmerited grace.

While I look to Him as my Savior from the *penalty*, may I know Him also as my Deliverer from the *power* of sin. I have to lament that so often I have yielded to its solicitations — that my heart, a temple of the Holy Spirit, has been so often profaned and dishonored by the "accursed thing," marring my spiritual joy, and sorely interrupting communion with the Lord I love. Give me grace to exercise a godly jealousy over my traitor affections — to live nearer You — to have the magnet of my heart more centered on Yourself — to keep the eye of faith more steadily on Jesus — to live more habitually under "the powers of the world to come." You know my *besetting* sin — the plague of my heart, which so often leads to a guilty estrangement. Lord, cut down this root of bitterness. Let me nail it to Your cross. Let me be ever on the watchtower, ready to resist the first assault of the enemy. Let it be to me at once a precept and a promise — "Sin shall not have dominion over you." Oh show me that my strength to repel temptation is in Jesus alone. Put me in the cleft of the rock when the hurricane is passing by. May I be as willing to surrender all for my Savior — my heart sins and life sins — as He willingly surrendered His all for me. May I be enabled to say, "Lord I am Yours."

Every idol I utterly abolish. Save me, blessed Savior from a deceitful heart and a seductive world. Let me see more and more the beauties of holiness. Let me ever be basking in the rays of Your love — approaching nearer and nearer You, the "Sun of my soul." May Your loveliness and glory eclipse all created beams and may I look forward with bounding heart to that time when all that helps to lighten up earth's pathway shall be obscured in the shadow of death, and I shall be ushered into the glories of that better and brighter scene, where "the sun shall no more go down, neither shall the moon withdraw itself, but where the Lord my God shall be my everlasting light."

And what I ask for myself, I desire in behalf of those near and dear to me. "Sanctify them wholly." May they, too, crucify sin, and "die daily." May this be the happy history of all of us — "Being made free from sin, and having become the servants of God, we have our fruit unto holiness, and the end everlasting life." Amen.

"Let the morning bring me word of Your unfailing love, for I have put my trust in You. Show me the way I should go, for to You I lift up my soul."

13th Morning
FOR GROWTH IN HOLINESS

"In the morning, O Lord, You hear my voice; in the morning I lay my requests before You — and wait in expectation."

"Grow in grace." — 2 Pet. 3:18

O God, draw near to me in fullness in Your great mercy. Another peaceful morning has dawned upon me. May it be mine to know the happiness of those who walk all the day in the light of Your countenance.

O best and kindest of Beings, teach me to know, amid the smiles and the frowns, the joys and the sorrows, of an ever-changing world, what it is to have an unchanging refuge and portion in You. I can mourn no blank, I can feel no solitude, when I have Your presence and love. If I have nothing beside — stripped and divested of every other blessing — I have the richest of all, if I am at peace with God.

I desire to dwell with devout contemplation on the infinite loveliness of Your moral nature. Lord, I long to have this guilty, erring soul, molded and fashioned in increasing conformity to Your blessed mind and will. Let my great concern henceforth be, to love and serve and please You more and more. May all Your dealings with me, of whatever kind they be, contribute in promoting this growth in holiness. May *prosperity* draw forth a perpetual thank-offering of praise for unmerited mercies. May *adversity* purify away the dross of worldliness and sin. May every day be finding the power of sin weaker and weaker, and the dominion of grace stronger and stronger. Living under the powers of a world to come, may I look forward with joyful expectation to the time when sin shall no longer impede my spiritual growth — when Satan shall be disarmed of his power, and my own heart of its deceitfulness — when every faculty of a glorified and exalted nature shall be enlisted in Your service in a world of eternal joy.

O blessed Advocate within the veil — You who are even now interceding for Your tried and tempted saints, "that their faith fail not" — Impart to me a constant supply of Your promised grace. Not only sprinkle my heart with Your blood, but conquer it by Your love. Fill me with deep contrition for an erring past — inspire me with purposes of new obedience for the future. May I know, in my sweet experience, that "Your yoke is easy and Your burden light" — that, growing in holiness, I am growing in happiness too. Give me an increasing tenderness of conscience about sin — lead me, with more filial devotedness, to cultivate a holy fear of offending so gracious a Father. Habitually realizing my new covenant relationship to You, may I ever be ready to exclaim, with joyful sincerity "O Lord, truly I am Your servant!"

Revive, blessed God, Your own work everywhere. "Take to Yourself Your great power, and reign." Remove all hardness and blindness of heart — all contempt of Your Word. May it have free course and be glorified.

Bless my dear friends. However far separated from one another, we can ever meet at the same throne of the heavenly grace, pleading the same "exceeding great and precious promises." May we all be following the same path of grace now, and meet amid the endless joys of glory hereafter. And all I ask is for Jesus' sake. Amen.

"Let the morning bring me word of Your unfailing love, for I have put my trust in You. Show me the way I should go, for to You I lift up my soul."

14th Morning
FOR VICTORY OVER THE WORLD

"In the morning, O Lord, You hear my voice; in the morning I lay my requests before You — and wait in expectation."
"Everyone born of God overcomes the world." — 1 John 5:4

O eternal, everlasting God, You are glorious in holiness, fearful in praises, continually doing wonders. Heaven and earth are full of the majesty of Your glory. You, the almighty keeper of Israel, never slumber. There is not the moment I am away from your wakeful vigilance. In the defenseless hours of sleep, as well as amid life's activities and toils, You are ever the same — "compassing my path and my lying down, and intimately acquainted with all my ways."

I rejoice to think that I have the assurance of such unwearying watchfulness and care, in a world "lying in wickedness." Blessed Jesus, in the world You have forewarned me to expect tribulation, but, nevertheless, I will "be of good cheer, for you have overcome the world." You have traversed its wilderness-depths — You have passed through the shadow of its darkest valley. I cannot dread what You have trodden and conquered.

But, alas! I have to mourn that the world which crucified You should be so much loved by me — that its pleasures should be so fascinating — its pursuits so engrossing. Wean me from it. Break its alluring spell. Strip it of its counterfeit charms. Discover to me, its hollowness — the treachery of its promises — the precariousness of its best blessings — the fleeting nature of its most enduring friendship. I take comfort in the thought, "The Lord God is a sun and shield." The world has deceived me, but You never have. Guide me by Your counsel. Savior-God, let me come up from the wilderness leaning on Your arm, exulting, amid its legion-foes, that greater is He who is with me than all those who can be against me.

O You who, in Your last prayer on earth, did so touchingly say of Your pilgrim people, "These are in the world;" still bend Your pitying eye upon me, as I travel, burdened with sin and sorrow, through the valley of tears. So "sanctify me through Your truth," that, though *in* the world, I may not be *of* it — not conformed to its sinful practices and lying vanities. Bring me to say, with regard to all in it that was once so fascinating, "My soul is even as a weaned child." With my face Zionward, may I declare plainly that I seek "a better country."

Grant that this day, in all my worldly communion, I may have the realizing sense of Your presence and nearness. May I set a watch on my heart, and keep the door of my lips. May cherished feelings of love and devotion to You be intermingled with all life's duties and engagements. May I know that a simple faith in Jesus is the great secret of victory over the world. Oh, may the trembling magnet of my vacillating affections be ever pointing to Him, and then I shall be made "more than conqueror."

Through His all-prevailing merits and advocacy, hear my prayer. In His most precious blood, forgive all my sins. By His indwelling grace, sanctify my nature, that my whole body, soul, and spirit may be preserved blameless until His coming. Amen.

"Let the morning bring me word of Your unfailing love, for I have put my trust in You. Show me the way I should go, for to You I lift up my soul."

15th Morning
FOR DEEPER VIEWS OF SELF

"In the morning, O Lord, You hear my voice; in the morning I lay my requests before You — and wait in expectation."

"Search me, O God, and know my heart." — Psalm 139:23

O eternal, everlasting God, who have once more enlightened my eyes, and allowed me not to sleep the sleep of death, bestow upon me this day the riches of Your grace and love. Morning after morning is dawning upon me, with new tokens of Your mercy. Oh, may these be bringing me nearer the glorious day which is to know no night — that eternal noon-tide when all shadows and darkness are forever to flee away!

Lord, I am unworthy to come into Your presence, and yet I have to mourn that I do not feel this deep unworthiness as I ought. I am unwilling to see into the unknown depths of my sin. I do not know myself. I have no depressing consciousness of the desperate wickedness of my own evil heart. I have buried many past transgressions in oblivion. I have deluded myself with the thought, that many were too trivial and unimportant to incur Your disapproval. Even any imperfect good which Your grace has enabled me to perform, I have been too prone to take the merit to myself, instead of ascribing all the praise to You. There has been pride in my humility. There have been mingled motives in my best services. My best resolutions have been fitful and transient. My purest and most unselfish actions could not stand the scrutiny of Your eye. The holiest day I ever spent, were I to be judged by it, would condemn me.

O You who "searches Jerusalem with lighted candles," "search my heart." Bring me to the publican's place of penitential sorrow, exclaiming, in self-renouncing humility, "God be merciful to me a sinner!"

I would seek to make a more entire and undivided surrender of all I am and have to You. Give me such a dreadful and affecting sense of my vileness, that I may never feel safe but when close to the atoning Fountain, drawing out of it hourly supplies. May mine be a daily heart and self and sin crucifixion — an eternal severance from those bosom traitors which have so long separated between me and my God. Make me more zealous for Your honor and glory — "Cleanse the thoughts of my heart, by the inspiration of Your Holy Spirit" — "Let no iniquity obtain dominion over me." But may it be my daily ambition to become more like You, reflecting more of the image, and imbibing more of the spirit, of my Divine Redeemer, that thus the atmosphere of holiness and of heaven may be diffused all around me. May my own soul be pervaded with lofty and purified aspirations. May I be enabled to exhibit to the world the felt happiness of close walking with God.

And gracious Father, "send forth Your light and Your truth" to a darkened world. May Your own ancient people be speedily gathered in with the fullness of the Gentile nations, that all ends of the earth may see the salvation of God.

Bless all my dear friends, near or distant. May they have the heritage of those who fear Your name. Defend them now by Your mighty power, and at last number them with Your saints in glory everlasting. Amen.

"Let the morning bring me word of Your unfailing love, for I have put my trust in You. Show me the way I should go, for to You I lift up my soul."

16th Morning
FOR BRIGHTER VIEWS OF JESUS

"In the morning, O Lord, You hear my voice; in the morning I lay my requests before You — and wait in expectation."

"That I may know Him." — Phil. 3:10

Blessed Jesus! — Sun of my soul! — Light of my life! — Shine upon me this morning with the "brightness of Your rising." May I enjoy this day union and communion with You. May a sense of Your favor pervade all its duties, sanctify its blessings, and lighten its trials. May it be to me the sweetest and holiest of all thoughts, that You are ever with me — that, though unseen to the eye of sense, the eye of faith can discern Your gracious presence and the manifestations of Your nearness and love. May the realized assurance, that You are thus at my side, dispel every misgiving, and dry every tear. May I hear You, even now, saying to me, "Lo, I am with you" — I am with you *now* — I shall be with you *"always"* — and when the world is ended "I will" that you "be with me where I am, that you may behold my glory!"

O adorable Savior, how sadly is Your beauty obscured from my view, by reason of my own sin! How feebly do I apprehend the mystery of Your love — the glories of Your person — the perfection of Your atonement! Hide me in the clefts of the rock, and while there, "I beseech You, show me Your glory." May every fresh glimpse of "the great love with which You have loved me" rebuke the lukewarmness of my own. May I covet a closer walk with You. May my existence be one continued Emmaus journey — its hours passing joyfully by, because happy in the presence and converse of a risen Redeemer. Blessed Jesus, "abide with me," for the day is "far spent." Let me walk with You in newness of life. May I breathe Your spirit of holy submission — of cheerful obedience — of patience under injuries. May I not repine at bearing the cross, so meekly borne for me; nor murmur at my trials, when I think of Yours. May I be enabled to make every lineament of Your spotless character my daily study, so as gradually to be transformed into the same image, from glory to glory — looking forward to that blessed time when I shall see You without one stain of remaining sin to dim the contemplation, and when I shall be permitted to bathe in the ocean of Your eternal love.

I thank You for the mercies of the past night. Allow me to consider every new day a fresh gift of Your dying grace — to regard all its hours as redeemed hours — every moment as "bought with a price." May these days, and hours, and moments, thus stamped with the cross, be consecrated more than ever to Your praise.

Again I beseech You, "abide with me." "Where You go I will go, and where You dwell I will dwell." Abide with me from morning to evening, and from evening to morning again. "Without You I cannot live" — "without You I dare not die." Living or dying, Lord, I would seek to be Yours.

Forgive all my many sins, and when the feeble glimpses of a feeble love on earth are at an end, bring me at last to enjoy brighter views of You in glory everlasting. Amen.

"Let the morning bring me word of Your unfailing love, for I have put my trust in You. Show me the way I should go, for to You I lift up my soul."

17th Morning
FOR NEARER VIEWS OF HEAVEN

"In the morning, O Lord, You hear my voice; in the morning I lay my requests before You — and wait in expectation."
"They shall behold the land that is very far off. "Isaiah 33:17

O God, in the multitude of Your mercies I am again permitted to see the light of a new day. With another rising morn scatter all the clouds of sin and unbelief from my soul. Unfold to my view bright glimpses of Yourself — sweet foretastes of those joys which "eye has not seen, nor ear heard."

Here, Lord, I have "no continuing city" — change is my portion in this the house of my pilgrimage — I would not desire to live here always. I am "willing rather to be absent from the body and to be present with the Lord." Wean me from this uncertain world. Bring me to live under the powers of a world to come. I rejoice to think of the happy myriads already in glory — "clothed in white robes, with palms in their hands" — safe in the presence of the Master they love, with every tear-drop wiped away. I rejoice to know that the blood and grace to which they owe their crowns are still free as ever. Oh, may I be enabled, with some good measure of triumphant assurance, to say, "Henceforth there is laid up for *me* a crown of righteousness, which the Lord, the righteous Judge, shall give me at that day." May the thought of that endless, sinless, sorrowless immortality reconcile me to all earth's severest discipline. Let me not murmur under the heaviest cross in the prospect of such a crown. Let me not refuse to pass cheerfully through the hottest furnace which is to refine and purify me for this "exceeding weight of glory;" but bear with calm serenity whatever You see fit to lay upon me. "Weeping may endure for a night, but joy comes in the morning."

Lord, grant that the approach of eternity may urge me to greater diligence in Your service. May I have my loins girded and my lamp burning. May I spend each day, and *this* day, as if it were to be my last. When the shadows of evening gather around me, may I feel that I have spent a day for God. Nearer a dying hour — may it find me nearer heaven.

What I ask for myself I would seek in behalf of all my beloved friends. Sprinkle each heart with the blood of the covenant. May every eye be directed to Jesus, and every footstep be pointing heavenward. Though severed from one another now, may we not be found gathered in different bundles on the great reaping-day of judgment.

Lord, unite Your own people more and more. Why should we be guilty of such sad estrangements, crossing and recrossing one another on life's highway with alien and jealous looks, when professing to be sprinkled with the same blood, to bear the same name, and be heirs of the same inheritance? Let me live near to Jesus, and then I shall live near all His people, looking forward to that blessed time when we shall see eye to eye and heart to heart — no jarring or discordant note to mar the everlasting ascription of "blessing, and honor, and glory and power, to Him who sits upon the throne, and to the Lamb, forever and ever." Amen.

"Let the morning bring me word of Your unfailing love, for I have put my trust in You. Show me the way I should go, for to You I lift up my soul."

18th Morning
FOR WEANEDNESS FROM THE CREATURE

"In the morning, O Lord, You hear my voice; in the morning I lay my requests before You — and wait in expectation."
"There is none upon earth that I desire besides You." — Psalm 73:25

O Lord, blessed fountain of all happiness and joy, draw near to me this morning in Your great mercy. All creature-comforts are emanations from You. Your favor is life — Your displeasure is worse than death. In losing You, we lose our all — in having You, we can lack nothing.

I have to acknowledge, with shame and confusion of face, that I have not thus been seeking my true enjoyment in You. I have been in pursuit of fleeting shadows, which one by one have eluded my grasp. I have been worshiping and serving the creature more than the Creator, who is "God over all, blessed forevermore." Lord, bring me to see that nothing short of Yourself can satisfy the longings and desires of my immortal nature. Wean me from what is perishable. Let me reverentially acquiesce in whatever means You may employ to bring my wandering heart back to You, O you who are the alone-satisfying portion of my soul. Rather, Lord, would I submit to the hardest discipline than listen to the withering words, "Ephraim is joined to idols: let him alone." Let me feel that Your presence and love can compensate for the loss of all earthly joys. As prop after prop which has gladdened my pilgrimage totters and falls, may I know what it is to "dwell in the secret place of the Most High, and to abide under the shadow of the Almighty." As You are ever proclaiming over creature-confidence, "Dust you are, and into dust shall you return," may I know what it is to cleave to One who is better and surer than the nearest and dearest on earth — the Friend that never fails, and never wearies, and never dies — "Jesus Christ, the same yesterday, and to day and forever."

Blessed Savior, I cast my every care on You. You are noting now on Your throne, the pangs and sorrows of every burdened heart. All other love is imperfect. All other sympathy is selfish but Yours.

May my affections be consecrated to You. May it be my joy to serve You — my privilege to follow You, and, if necessary, to suffer with You. May every cross lose its bitterness by having You at my side. May I feel that nothing but absence from You can create a real loss in my heart. Your presence takes the sting from all afflictions, and imparts security in the midst of all troubles. Living or dying, may I be Yours.

Sprinkle me this new morning with the blood of the covenant. May I feel all throughout the day the joy of being reconciled to God. May my heart be made a little sanctuary of praise. May I breathe the atmosphere of heaven. May God Himself be so enthroned in my affections, that I may be enabled to say, in comparison with Him, of all that the world can give, "There is none upon the earth that I desire beside You."

Heavenly Father, I leave all that belongs to me to You — "Undertake for them." Bless them and make them blessings. "Hide them under the shadow of Your wings" until earth's "calamities be over." Hear this my morning supplication; and when you hear, forgive. And all I ask is for Jesus' sake. Amen.

"Let the morning bring me word of Your unfailing love, for I have put my trust in You. Show me the way I should go, for to You I lift up my soul."

19th Morning
FOR LOWLINESS OF MIND

"In the morning, O Lord, You hear my voice; in the morning I lay my requests before You — and wait in expectation."

"He gives grace to the humble." — 1 Pet. 5:5

O God, You are "the high and lofty One who inhabits eternity." There is no being truly great but You. All other excellence and glory is derived — Yours is underived. All else is finite — Yours is infinite. The burning seraph nearest Your throne is the humblest of all Your creatures, because he gets the nearest view of the majesty of Your glory.

Lord, fill my soul this morning with suitable views of Your greatness, and a humbling estimate of my own nothingness. I would lie low at Your feet — in wonder and amazement that dust and ashes should be permitted to approach that Being whom angels worship with folded wings, and in whose sight the very "heavens are not clean." Repress every proud, self-glorifying imagination.

Let me feel I cannot abase myself enough in Your presence. "Lord, I am vile; what can I answer You?" My best thoughts, how polluted! — my best services, how imperfect! — my best affections, how lukewarm! — my best prayers how cold! — my best hours, were I judged by them, how would I be condemned!

I desire to take refuge at the cross of a crucified Savior. Here, Lord, give me that grace You have promised to the lowly. Self-renouncing and sin-renouncing, I would seek to be exalted only in Jesus, crying out, "God be merciful to me a sinner!" In broken-heartedness of soul, I mourn the past. Distrustful of the future, I look only to You. Full of my own unworthiness, I turn to the infinitely worthy One. I seek to be washed in His blood — sanctified by His Spirit — guided by His counsel — depending on Him for every supply of grace — and feeling that without Him I must perish.

May I take the humility and gentleness of Jesus as my pattern. Like Him, may I be meek and lowly in heart. Give me grace to avoid ostentation and pride, haughtiness and vanity, envy and uncharitableness. "In lowliness of mind may I esteem others better than myself." Let me realize every moment that I am a pensioner on Divine bounty — that I am alike "for temporals and spirituals" dependent on You — and that it well becomes me to be "clothed with humility." Oh, let me meekly and submissively lose my own will in Yours, in childlike teachableness, saying — "What will You have me to do?" May no murmur escape my lips at Your dealings. May this lowliness of spirit lead me rather to wonder at Your sparing mercy, that the great and holy Being I have provoked so long by my rebellion has not "cut me down."

Bless all connected to me by endearing bonds. May nature's ties be made doubly strong by those of covenant grace. Bless Your cause and kingdom in the world. May Your Spirit descend "like rain upon the mown grass, and showers that water the earth."

I commit myself to You, and to the word of Your grace. Guide me this day by Your counsel. May I spend it as if it were to be my last. And when my last day does arrive, may it be to me the eve of a happy eternity. And all I ask is for Jesus' sake. Amen.

"Let the morning bring me word of Your unfailing love, for I have put my trust in You. Show me the way I should go, for to You I lift up my soul."

20th Morning
FOR SIMPLICITY OF FAITH

"In the morning, O Lord, You hear my voice; in the morning I lay my requests before You — and wait in expectation."
"Only believe." — Mark 5:36

O eternal, ever-blessed Fountain of all light — Source of all happiness — "God of all grace" — look down upon me this morning with that love which "You bear to Your own," as I venture anew into Your sacred presence. Let me enjoy a sweet season of fellowship with You. Let the world be shut out, and may I feel alone with God. "Under the shadow of Your wings would I rejoice."

I come in the nothingness of the creature, standing alone in the fullness of Jesus. I come, "just as I am, without one plea" — as a sinner, and as the "chief of sinners" — to You, almighty Savior. I seek to disown all creature confidence, and, with all the burden of my guilt, to cast myself, for time and for eternity, at Your feet. "Lord, save me, else I perish." I cannot stand in myself. I can stand only in Him who has stood so willingly a Surety for me — who is still at the right hand of the Majesty in the heavens, presenting my name, and my prayers, and my plea, before the throne. I *have* no other confidence, and I *need* no other. Jesus, I am complete in You. Let me not look inwardly on myself, where there is everything to sink me in despondency and dismay; but let me look with the undivided and unwavering eye of faith to Your bleeding sacrifice. I rejoice to think of the many robes in the Church triumphant Your blood has already made white. I rejoice to know that the same blood is free as ever — the same invitation is addressed as ever — the promise and the Promiser remain "faithful" as ever — "Him who comes to me I will in no wise cast out."

Lord, I come — I plead Your word. I come, irrespective of all I am, and all I have been. Magnify Your grace in me. Show me my utter beggary and wretchedness by nature — that every step to glory is a step of grace; and while, with childlike faith, I rest on the finished work of Jesus, may I have the same simple trust and confidence in all His dealings towards me. May I feel that the Shepherd of Israel cannot lead me wrong — that His own way must be the safest and the best. Lord, "undertake for me" — "I will follow You to prison and to death." Take me — lead me — use me, as You see good. If I need chastisement, give me chastisement. If I need rebuke, let me not complain under the rod. Let me trust a Father's word — a Father's love — a Father's discipline. "Though You slay me, yet will I trust in You."

And as for myself, so for all dear to me. I pray that it may please You, of Your infinite mercy, to visit them with Your salvation — to guide them by Your counsel — to overrule all life's changes and vicissitudes and trials for their well-being, and at last to bring them safe to Your eternal kingdom, through Jesus Christ — to whom, with You, O Father, and You, O eternal Spirit, three in one in covenant for our redemption, be ascribed, all blessing, and honor, and glory, and praise, world without end. Amen.

"Let the morning bring me word of Your unfailing love, for I have put my trust in You. Show me the way I should go, for to You I lift up my soul."

21st Morning
FOR CONSISTENCY OF WALK

"In the morning, O Lord, You hear my voice; in the morning I lay my requests before You — and wait in expectation."

"Walk worthy of the Lord unto all pleasing." — Col. 1:10

O Lord, You are the heart-searching and the thought-trying God. To You all hearts are open — from You no secrets are hidden. Cleanse the thoughts of my heart this day, by the inspiration of Your Holy Spirit. I would seek to begin its hours with You. May all its business and employments be perfumed with the fragrance of "the morning sacrifice."

O You who are the great origin and end of all things, be to me the Alpha and the Omega of my daily being. May I feel existence to be a blank without You. May I feel that I can only be truly happy when a sense of Your favor and friendship, and love is sweetly intermingled with life's duties — thus lessening every burden — hallowing every trial — diminishing every cross!

I come to You once more, an unworthy sinner, to cast myself at my Savior's feet. What am I, that You should have borne with me so long! The ax "laid at the root of the trees" might long ago have cut me down; but I, a guilty cumberer, am still spared. The retrospect of existence, while a retrospect of patience and forbearance on Your part, is one of mournful rebellion and ingratitude on mine. I have had a "name to live," but how much spiritual death in my best frames! I have had a form of godliness; how little have I lived out and acted out its power! More careful have I been to *appear* to be a Christian than really to *be* a Christian. How much unevenness in my walk — how much proclaimed and professed by the lip has been undone and denied in the life!

I come this morning to ask anew for mercy to pardon, and grace to help me. Especially give me the grace of a holy consistency, doing all for Your glory, having boldness to speak for You in the world. May my walk and conversation be the living evidence and expression of the sincerity and reality of the inner life.

For this end may I live more on Jesus. May my life be "hidden with Christ in God." May I grow more and more out of myself and *into* my living Head. Self-humbled and self-emptied, may I be ever resorting to the all-fullness of an all-sufficient Savior. May this be my habitual feeling — "Without Him I can do nothing." May this be my constant prayer — "Help me, Savior, or I die."

May I be enabled this day, in His strength, to do something for God. However lowly my lot, however humble my abilities, may I feel, Lord, that You have work for me in Your vineyard. Let me not bury my talent in the earth; may I "occupy it until You come," that "You may receive Your own with interest."

Have mercy on Your whole Church. Pour out on all its members and office-bearers the spirit of meekness and zeal, of power and love, and of a sound mind. May "Holiness to the Lord" be written on its portals!

Hasten the blessed period when the love of Jesus, being enthroned in every heart and every Church, "we all shall be one." And all I ask is for the Redeemer's sake. Amen.

"Let the morning bring me word of Your unfailing love, for I have put my trust in You. Show me the way I should go, for to You I lift up my soul."

22nd Morning
FOR SINGLENESS OF EYE

"O Lord, in the morning will I direct my prayer unto You."
"This one thing I do." — Phil. 3:13

My Father in heaven, teach me, in childlike faith and confidence, to draw near this morning to Your throne of grace. Give me the blessed influences of Your Holy Spirit, that I may wait on You undisturbed by worldly distractions, and enter on the duties of another day with my mind "stayed on God."

Blessed Jesus! — You who so freely gave Yourself a ransom for many — save me, else I perish! I have no peace but in Your pardoning, reconciling love. May Your blood and righteousness be to me "a glorious dress," arrayed in which I may now and forever stand fearless and undismayed. I bless You, O God, if I have in any degree felt the preciousness of the Savior and His adaptation to all the needs and weaknesses of my sinful, and sorrowful, and tempted nature. I thank You if You have already hidden me in the clefts of the smitten Rock. My prayer is, that You may keep me there — that I may lean upon Jesus more than ever, and seek my happiness more exclusively in His service. May I every morning be drawn more closely by the cords of His love, and be led to fight more faithfully under His banner.

Oh for greater singleness of aim! — more self-emptying and self-abasing — that He may be all in all! Lord, I am conscious often of mingled motives, that would not stand the test of Your pure eye and Your holy Word! How often do I forfeit the joys of assurance by admitting rival claimants to the throne of my affections! How often are the surpassing interests and glories of eternity dimmed and obscured by the engrossing things of time and of sense! How mixed with imperfection and earthliness and self-seeking are my best attempts to serve You! If weighed in the balance, how would my holiest services be found lacking!

Give me more of this unity and simplicity of purpose. Give me to make salvation more the one thing needful. Let all other love be subordinated to Yours. Be my "chief joy." May Your service be my delight. May my heart become a little sanctuary, where the incense of praise and love and thanksgiving is ascending continually. May it glow with holy zeal to promote Your cause, and testify of Your grace. Remembering all that You have done for me, may I be animated to make a more entire consecration and surrender of all I am and have to Your glory.

Let me feel that whatever my rank or station or circumstances are, I have some mission to perform for You. How often do You choose "the foolish things of the world to confound the things that are mighty!" Let me not think my talent too trifling to trade upon. May I "occupy it until my Lord comes." Let me not squander fleeting moments, or forego fleeting opportunities. "The night is coming, when none of us can work." Enable me now, bowing at Your mercy-seat, to replenish anew my empty vessel with the oil of Your grace, that the lamp of faith may be kept burning brightly all the day. All that I ask is for Jesus' sake. Amen.

"Let the morning bring me word of Your unfailing love, for I have put my trust in You. Show me the way I should go, for to You I lift up my soul."

23rd Morning
FOR FILIAL NEARNESS

"In the morning, O Lord, You hear my voice; in the morning I lay my requests before You — and wait in expectation."

"Abba, Father." — Rom. 8:15

Most blessed God, I rejoice that I can look up to You, the mightiest of all beings, and call You by that name, which may well dispel all misgivings, and hush all disquietudes — "My *Father* who is in heaven."

Father, I have sinned against heaven and in Your sight. The kindest of earthly parents could not so long have borne with ingratitude and waywardness like mine. Long before now You might righteously have driven me an exile and a cast away from Your presence. But the voice of parental mercy is not silenced. The hand of parental patience and love is "stretched out still." In the midst of deserved wrath, this is Your own gracious declaration, "I will be a Father to you!"

I mourn my grievous departures — my repeated declensions — my heinous ingratitude. Oh, let me no longer live in this state of guilty estrangement — forfeiting all the joys of a Father's tenderness, the sunshine of a Father's smile. May I know what it is for the soul, orphaned, and portionless, and friendless by nature, to repose in the security of Your covenant-love. May I be enabled to enjoy more and more, every day, holy filial nearness to the mercy-seat — there unburdening into Your ear all my needs and trials — my sorrows and perplexities — my backslidings and sins. Give me grace to bow with childlike submission to a Father's will — to bear without a murmur a Father's rod — to hear in every dealing, joyous or sorrowful, a Father's voice — and when death comes, to have every fear dispelled by listening to a Father's summons — "Today you shall be with me in paradise."

Jesus, blessed Elder Brother! "in whom the whole family in heaven and earth is named," may I be enabled to imitate Your example of holy resignation to Your Father's will. May the cup of bitterest earthly sorrow be taken into my hands with Your own breathing of devout submission — "This cup which You give me to drink, shall I not drink it? Even so, Father, for so it seems good in Your sight." It is my comfort, blessed Lord, to know, that while the best of earthly parents may err, You, the unerring God, never can. In Your most mysterious dealings there is wisdom. In Your roughest voice there is mercy.

Adorable Redeemer, all these filial blessings and adoption-privileges I owe to You. It is Your precious blood-shedding which has "set me among the children" — it is that which still keeps me there. Anew this day would I repair to Your cross — anew would I supplicate that the Holy Spirit, the Divine Comforter, would be sent forth into my heart, enabling me to cry, "Abba, Father." May the thought of this blessed trust in You, support me amid life's fitful changes and transient friendships, and may I be enabled to dwell with holy delight on that glorious time, when, no longer an exiled pilgrim in a strange land, I shall be received at the gates of glory with a Father's welcome — "*Son*, you are ever with me, and all that I have is yours."

I commend myself and all near and dear to me, this day, to Your fatherly care and keeping. And all I ask is for Jesus' sake. Amen.

"Let the morning bring me word of Your unfailing love, for I have put my trust in You. Show me the way I should go, for to You I lift up my soul."

24th Morning
FOR RESTORATION TO FAVOR

"In the morning, O Lord, You hear my voice; in the morning I lay my requests before You — and wait in expectation."
"Restore to me the joy of Your salvation." — Psalm 51:12

O God, another morning has dawned upon me. "Better Sun of righteousness" — with the brightness of Your rising may all the shadows of guilt and sin be dispersed. I come, weak and weary, guilty and heavy-laden, to You, beseeching You to bend Your pitying eye upon me — to deal not with me as I have deserved, nor reward me according to my iniquity. Blessed Jesus, look upon me. In You may I be pitied, pardoned, and forgiven!

I have erred and strayed from Your way as a lost sheep. I have wandered from the home of my God. I have been seeking my happiness in what is shadowy and unreal. The world and its delusive hopes have been preferred to You. My heart, which ought ever to be a little altar and sanctuary of praise, has burned with false incense. Your love and glory have not maintained their paramount place in my affections. I have righteously forfeited "the joys of Your salvation." My only marvel is, that, as a wandering star, You have not left me to drift onwards to the blackness of darkness forever. O leave me not to perish! I mourn my wanderings. In leaving You, I feel I have left my Best Friend. I have caused an aching void in this heart, which the world, with all its joys and riches and pleasures, can never fill. I cannot have one hour of happiness, if mingled with the thought that I am estranged from You, my God. Blissful hours of Your favor I once enjoyed, come sorrowfully to my remembrance; and, though the cup of earthly happiness be full to the brim, I have still to breathe the prayer — "Oh that it were with me as in months past, when the candle of the Lord did shine!"

"Restore to me the joy of Your salvation." Leave me not in this state of distance and alienation. "O Lord, I beseech You, deliver my soul." Snap these chains of earthliness that are still binding me to the dust, that, on the wings of faith, I may soar upwards, and find rest and quietude where alone it can be found — in Your renewed love and favor. May past backslidings drive me more to Your grace. Nothing in myself, may I find and feel that my all in all is in You. Reveal to me my own emptiness, and the overflowing fullness of Jesus. May I every day see more of His matchless excellencies — His incomparable loveliness — the sweets of His service — that I may never feel tempted to wander from His fold, and carefully avoid all that would risk the forfeiture of that favor in which indeed is "life."

Lord, let me know *this* day something of this happiness. Let me not be content with the *name* to live. Let religion be with me a real thing — let it be everything — life-influencing, sin-subduing, self-renouncing. Let me diffuse all around me the happy glow of a spirit that feels at peace with God.

And now, Lord, what do I wait for? "My hope" for myself, my friends, and all for whom I ought to pray, "is in You." Listen to these my supplications; and all I ask is for Jesus' sake. Amen.

"Let the morning bring me word of Your unfailing love, for I have put my trust in You. Show me the way I should go, for to You I lift up my soul."

25th Morning
FOR A PILGRIM SPIRIT

"In the morning, O Lord, You hear my voice; in the morning I lay my requests before You — and wait in expectation."
"And confessed that they were strangers and pilgrims on the earth." — Heb. 11:13

O God, again, in the multitude of Your mercies, You are permitting me to approach the footstool of Your throne. I am another day nearer death — oh, may I be a day nearer You! With a new morning's dawn may I hear the pilgrim summons — "Arise, for this is not your rest." Before I mingle with the world, give me to feel I am not *of* it, but born *from* above, and *for* above; and cherishing more of a pilgrim spirit, may my prayer and watchword be — "I desire a better country."

Lord, I bless You for the rich provision You have made for the wilderness journey — for all Your mercies, temporal, providential, and spiritual. Forbid that the many gifts of Your love should draw me away from Yourself, the bountiful Giver, or obliterate the solemn impression — "I am a stranger with You and a sojourner, as all my fathers were." May I "use the world without abusing it." By the varied discipline of Your providence, may I be led to feel that all my well-springs are in You. May the world's fascinations be becoming more powerless — sin more hated — holiness more loved — heaven more realized — God more "the exceeding joy" of my soul. Driven from all creature supports and earthly refuges, may Jesus be the prop and staff of my pilgrimage. When the world is bright, may I rest upon Him, and seek that He sanctify my prosperity. When the wilderness is dreary, and the way dark, may He hallow adversity. When friends are removed, may I feel that I have One left more faithful than the best of all earthly friends; and when death comes, and the pilgrim warfare ceases, leaning confidently on that same arm, may I enter the pilgrim's rest.

O adorable Savior! — You who were once Yourself a pilgrim — the lonely, weary, homeless, afflicted One — who had often no arm to lean upon, and no voice to cheer You — an outcast wanderer and sojourner in Your own creation — I rejoice to think that You have trodden all this wilderness-world before me — that You know its dreariest paths. I take comfort in the assurance that there is at the right hand of the Majesty on high, a fellow-Sufferer, who has drunk of every "brook in the way" — shed every tear of earthly sorrow — heaved every sigh of earthly suffering — and who, being Himself the "tried and tempted One," is able and willing to support every pilgrim who is tried and tempted too.

I beseech You this day to look down in great kindness on all my beloved friends. Seal to them a saving interest in Your great salvation. Wash them all in Your blood — sanctify them all by Your Spirit. May not one be missing on "the day when You make up Your jewels."

Pity a fallen world. Your Church is slumbering — the enemy is all vigilant — souls are perishing. Arise, Lord, and plead Your own cause. Promote greater unity and love and concord among Your own people. Let us be nearer Jesus, and then we shall be nearer one another. Give us all more of the single eye to Your glory. Make us more self-sacrificing — more heavenly-minded — more Savior-like. And all I ask is for Jesus' sake. Amen.

"Let the morning bring me word of Your unfailing love, for I have put my trust in You. Show me the way I should go, for to You I lift up my soul."

26th Morning
FOR PREPARATION FOR DEATH

"In the morning, O Lord, You hear my voice; in the morning I lay my requests before You — and wait in expectation."

"Prepare to meet your God." — Amos 4:12

O eternal, everlasting God — Author of my being — my continual, unwearied Benefactor — I desire to come anew this morning into Your presence, thanking You for Your sparing mercies. Instead of making my last night's pillow a pillow of death, I am again among the living to praise You. Oh that I were enabled to live every day, and to rise every morning, as if it were to be my last, as if my next waking were to be in the morning of immortality!

Lord, how little am I influenced and impressed by the solemn records of death all around me! Friend after friend is departing — the circle of acquaintance is narrowed. The proclamation is ever sounding with fresh emphasis in my ears, "You also be ready;" and yet how prone to disregard the solemn admonitions! how apt to peril my preparation on the peradventures of a dying hour! Blessed God, my prayer is, that I may have my loins girded and my lamp burning. Let me not wait to have my vessel replenished until the voice of the Bridegroom is heard and I am summoned to meet Him. May I now so repose my every confidence in Jesus, that the hour which to the unwary and unwatchful is one of darkness and terror, may be to me the eve of the blessed Sabbath of eternity — the threshold and the portal of a world of endless joy.

Lord, let me feel that "the sting of death is sin" — that, not until I get the blessed sense of all my sins cancelled and forgiven in the blood of the Surety, can I be ready for my departure. "To me to live, may it be Christ," that so "to die" may be great and eternal "gain." Let me be enabled, by faith in death's great Conqueror, to cultivate that holy familiarity with a dying hour, that I may be enabled, when it comes, to fall sweetly "asleep in Jesus," and to hear His voice of love saying, "It is I, don't be afraid."

Look in mercy on the multitudes who are content to live on, unfit and unprepared for their great change. Awaken them to a sense of their guilt and peril. Show them their affecting need of Jesus — that time is wasting and eternity is hastening — that, "as the tree falls, so must it lie."

I pray for the heathen who are perishing for lack of knowledge. Countenance and bless all the efforts of Your Church to disseminate among them the gospel of the grace of God. May Your missionary servants, who have gone with their lives in their hands to the dark places of the earth, experience a peace which the world knows not of. May they have many souls as their glory and joy and crown at the day of Christ's appearing.

Oh give us all grace, in our varied stations and relations in life, to do something for You. Let us not bury or hide our talents; but as members of a ransomed priesthood, may we lay our time, our opportunities, our substance, on Your altar, and seek to "show forth the praises of Him who has called us out of darkness into His marvelous light." And all I ask is for Jesus' sake. Amen.

"Let the morning bring me word of Your unfailing love, for I have put my trust in You. Show me the way I should go, for to You I lift up my soul."

27th Morning
FOR A JOYFUL RESURRECTION

"In the morning, O Lord, You hear my voice; in the morning I lay my requests before You — and wait in expectation."
"Awake and sing, you who dwell in dust." — Isa. 26:19

Gracious God, You have again dispersed the darkness of another natural night. Every rising earthly sun is bringing me nearer the gladdening day-break of immortality. O grant that, when the trumpet shall sound and the dead shall be raised, I may be ready to listen undismayed to the summons, "Behold, the Bridegroom comes, go out to meet Him."

My prayer is, that I may now be made partaker of the blessedness of the first resurrection from a death of sin. As one "alive from the dead," may I rise and walk with a living Savior in "newness of life," that thus I may at last share also in the more glorious resurrection of His ransomed saints, when His "dead men shall live," and together with His body "they shall arise," obeying the joyous mandate of their risen Head, "Awake and sing, you who dwell in the dust."

Blessed Jesus, I do rejoice to think of Your own triumphant rising from the tomb. I rejoice to be able to visit in thought Your vacant sepulcher, and to hear the glad tidings, "He is not here, He is risen!" "The Lord is risen!" — it is the blessed pledge and earnest of my own redemption from the power of the grave — that "because Christ lives, I shall live also." O may "my life be now hidden with Christ in God, so that when Christ, who is my life, shall appear, I may also appear with him in glory." Keep me ever in the frame I should wish to be found in when my Lord comes. May the lamp of faith and love be brightly burning. May it never be mine to be awakened, by the midnight cry, to the dreadful consciousness, "My lamp has gone out." May I rather be among the number of "waiting servants," who, when their Lord comes and knocks," are ready to open to Him immediately."

Impart to all near and dear to me this day the same spiritual and eternal blessings I ask for myself. May they, too, be united to Jesus — "planted in the likeness of His death," that they may be found also "in the likeness of His resurrection." May we all seek to bear an increasingly holy resemblance in love one to another, and to our great living Head, in whom the whole family in heaven and earth is named; and if for a little while separated by death, may we, on the great day of His appearing, be reunited in bonds that shall know no dissolution.

Hasten that blessed time when our world, so long groaning and travailing in pain, shall put on her resurrection attire, and exult in the glorious liberty of Your children. "Come, Lord Jesus; come quickly." "Why delay the wheels of Your chariot?"

Lord, I commend myself to You. Prepare me for living, prepare me for dying. Let me live near You in grace *now,* that I may live with You in glory *everlasting.* Let me be reconciled submissively to endure all that Your sovereign wisdom and love seem fit to appoint — looking forward, through the tears and sorrows of a weeping world, to that better day-spring, when "I shall behold Your face in righteousness," and be "satisfied, when I awake in Your likeness." And all I ask is for the Redeemer's sake. Amen.

"Let the morning bring me word of Your unfailing love, for I have put my trust in You. Show me the way I should go, for to You I lift up my soul."

28th Morning
FOR THE CONQUEST OF SATAN

"In the morning, O Lord, You hear my voice; in the morning I lay my requests before You — and wait in expectation."

"The God of peace shall bruise Satan under your feet shortly." — Rom. 16:20

O God, I bless You for the returning mercies of a new day. "I laid down and slept; I awoke, for the Lord sustained me. I will not be afraid of the ten thousands who have set themselves against me." Give me, I beseech You, Your fatherly protection and blessing, that all my thoughts may be ordered by You, and all my plans and purposes overruled by You, and all my joys hallowed by You, and all my sorrows sanctified by You. Keep me near Yourself. While I seek to realize, every hour of this day, the power and subtlety of my spiritual adversaries, may I rejoice in the assurance that greater is He who is with me than all those who can be against me — that, "though a host should encamp against me," with God on my side, "I need fear no evil."

I mourn the prevalence of sin, both in the world and in my own heart. Your creation still groans and travails under its power. "The Prince of the power of the air still works in the children of disobedience." "The whole world lies in the Wicked One." Often is Satan still "desiring to have me, that he might sift me as wheat" — "standing at my right hand to resist me" — to oppose my plea and damage my cause — sending some "thorn in the flesh to buffet me" — marring my peace, disturbing my joy, and hindering and impeding my spiritual growth and advancement. But, Lord, it is my comfort to know that there is in heaven a "stronger than the strong man" — that no time can impair or diminish the comfort of the assurance, "I have prayed for *you,* that your faith fail not." When Satan assaults, blessed Jesus, I will think of Your continual intercession. "Your hand is never shortened, that it cannot save."

May I ever have grace given me to "resist the devil, that he may flee from me" — to keep watchfully guarded every loophole of the heart. May I abstain from all appearance of evil, avoiding every place and every company where his unholy influences are likely to prevail. "Lead me not into temptation," and, if tempted, Lord, make a way of escape, that I may be able to bear it.

O adorable Intercessor within the veil, it is my comfort to know that, in Your season of humiliation on earth, You were "not ignorant of his devices." You also, of him, "suffered, being tempted," and You are therefore the more able "to aid those who are tempted." I rejoice to think that, exalted on Your mediatorial throne, You shall reign until Satan and every other enemy be put under Your feet, and until the kingdoms of this world (so long usurped by him) shall become the "one kingdom of our Lord and of His Christ."

Heavenly Father, take this day all my beloved friends under Your guardian care. May they dwell in the secret place of the Most High, and abide under the shadow of the Almighty. May they, too, be able to take up the triumphant challenge — "God is for us, who can be against us?" and when their earthly work and warfare is accomplished, may we all meet in that sinless world where Satan's seat no more can be found, and Satan's temptations shall no longer be felt or feared. And all that I ask is for Jesus' sake. Amen.

"Let the morning bring me word of Your unfailing love, for I have put my trust in You. Show me the way I should go, for to You I lift up my soul."

29th Morning
FOR THE OUTPOURING OF THE SPIRIT

"In the morning, O Lord, You hear my voice; in the morning I lay my requests before You — and wait in expectation."

"I will pour out my spirit upon all flesh." — Joel 2:28

O God, I desire this morning to approach with lowly reverence the footstool of Your throne, adoring and praising You for the rest of the past night, and the comforts and blessings of a new day. O holy, blessed, eternal Trinity, three persons, one God, have mercy upon me, and grant me Your benediction and love.

Most blessed Spirit of all grace, more especially would I at this time invoke Your presence and nearness. I acknowledge, with shame and confusion of face, how often I have grieved You by resisting Your gracious influences. How often have You pleaded with me by the voice of *Providence*, and yet I have turned a deaf ear to Your repeated warnings and remonstrances! You have spoken to me in *prosperity*, when the full cup demanded in return a heart full of gratitude. You have spoken to me in *adversity*, when, by the emptied cup and the broken cistern, You would have driven me from all earthly things, to the everlasting God Himself, as my only satisfying Portion. You have spoken to me by the terrors of the *law* and by the tender accents of *gospel* love, and yet I have continued to "spend my money for that which is not bread, and my labor for that which satisfies not." Long before now I might have exhausted Your patience. "It is of the Lord's mercies I am not consumed."

But "take not, O gracious God, Your Holy Spirit from me." Come, blessed Enlightener, Quickener, Sanctifier, and *inspire this dull cold heart*. Touched as with a live coal, may the flame of a holy love to You be rekindled on its altar. "Return, O Holy Dove, Messenger of rest," from the true ark of God. Give me grace to hate the sins which drove You away from this guilty breast. Breathe upon me and say, "Peace be to you; receive the Holy Spirit." Invigorate my languishing affections. May I realize my dependence on You for every pulsation of spiritual life. Without You I perish.

While I pray for this Blessed Agent in behalf of my own soul,

Lord, it is my earnest prayer that He may be poured out upon all flesh — that that time may soon come, when the rain of His gracious influences shall descend on a barren church and parched world. Hasten the Pentecost of the "latter day." Earth is at present but as the prophet's "valley of dry bones." Come, blessed Spirit of all grace, "breathe upon these dry bones, that they may live."

And may the same blessed and benevolent influences be shed on every heart that is dear to me. The Spirit of the Lord is not restricted. O my Father in heaven, have You not promised to give the Holy Spirit to those who ask You? I pray that all my beloved friends may become members of that mystical body of which Jesus is the living Head, so that the oil of anointing grace poured upon Him by the Spirit, and flowing down to the skirts of His garments, may be shared by His humblest and unworthiest members, O that each and all of our hearts may become living temples, in which the Holy Spirit dwells! May nothing that is unholy find admission there, but, "sealed with that Holy Spirit of promise, the earnest of our inheritance," may we be daily and habitually living in the expectation of eternal glory. Through Jesus Christ. Amen.

"Let the morning bring me word of Your unfailing love, for I have put my trust in You. Show me the way I should go, for to You I lift up my soul."

30th Morning
FOR THE UNION OF YOUR PEOPLE

"In the morning, O Lord, You hear my voice; in the morning I lay my requests before You — and wait in expectation."

"That they all may be one." — John 17:21

O God, the eternal Fountain of all excellence and glory! — through the one "new and living way" I desire this morning to approach You. Powerless in my own pleadings, I look up to the right hand of the throne of the Majesty in the heavens, to that "Prince who has power with God," and at all times "prevails." Guilty, I come to this guiltless Redeemer. Diseased, I come to this great Physician. Outcast, I come to Him who has promised that He will by no means "cast out." May His presence always be with me. May I know Him, and believe in Him, and rejoice in Him. May I feel that I need no other Savior — that He is all I require for life or for death — for time or for eternity.

I rejoice to think of the glorious multitude around Your throne — the trophies of Your grace — already wearing the white robe and the immortal palm. I rejoice to think of the blessed unity which pervades their glorified ranks: no note of discord disturbing their lofty harmonies — all seeing eye to eye, and heart to heart.

I lament the sad and mournful estrangement of Christian from Christian in Your Church below — that so many, treading the same heavenly journey, with the same glorious portals in view, should be following separate and diverse footpaths — that so many brethren in the Lord whose interchanges ought to be all love, should be looking coldly and censoriously on one another. How much ungodly jealousy, and heart-burning, and mutual recrimination, among Your professing people! How little of the spirit which of old provoked the testimony even of heathen gainsayers — "See how these Christians love one another!" O blessed "Author of peace and lover of concord," in Your mercy, pour out on Your Church on earth, a greater spirit of unity and brotherly-kindness, and charity. In Your mercy, heal the bleeding wounds of Your mystical body — casting over them the mantle of love. Bring us all, blessed Jesus, as individuals and as churches nearer Yourself, and then shall we be nearer one another. It is because of our distance from

You, the great Sun of Righteousness, the Source of light and life and peace, that we, as wandering stars are revolving in such devious and distant orbits. Give us to feel that we are all members of one mighty family, of which You are the glorious Head — that, though following diverse tracks, we are sheep of the same pasture, owning the same "Chief Shepherd" — that, though enrolled in different ranks, we are allies in the same great army, fighting under the banner of the same great Captain of salvation. O forbid that, in these "latter days" — in these times of trouble, and rebuke, and blasphemy, when "the enemy is coming in like a flood" — we should waste our strength on petty and puny dissensions! May we be led to merge the few points in which we differ, in the many in which we can unite.

Preserve me, good Lord, this day, from all uncharitableness. May I "judge not, that I be not judged." May I have Your favor resting upon me in all the day's duties, and Your love softening and sanctifying all its trials. May all my beloved friends be one with me in Jesus — one now, and one in glory everlasting. Amen.

"Let the morning bring me word of Your unfailing love, for I have put my trust in You. Show me the way I should go, for to You I lift up my soul."

31st Morning
FOR THE COMING OF YOUR KINGDOM

"In the morning, O Lord, You hear my voice; in the morning I lay my requests before You — and wait in expectation."

"May Your kingdom come." — Luke 11:2

O eternal, ever-blessed God, whose merciful kindness is new to me every morning — give me throughout this day that peace which the world cannot give. As the beams of the material sun are lighting up anew my earthly chamber, may the inner chamber of my soul be illuminated by a better and brighter radiance. Jesus! blessed Fountain of light, and life, and glory, disperse all the darkness of unbelief and sin. May Your presence and love hallow all my joys, and mitigate and sanctify all my sorrows.

Before I enter on the day's duties, sprinkle once again the lintels and doorposts of my heart with Your own most precious blood; may my inmost thoughts, and purposes, and desires, and affections be consecrated to that God whose property they are. May I have an increasing experience of the sweets of Your favor, and friendship, and love. With You, blessed Lord, I am rich, whatever else I lack; without You, I am poor, though I have the wealth of worlds beside. Take what You will away — but take not Yourself. Nothing can fill and satisfy the longings of my immortal nature but You — all worldly happiness and creature joys are poor substitutes for the inexhaustible source of all joy. Let me know what it is, amid the wreck of earthly refuges and hopes, to exult in the persuasion, "The Lord lives; and blessed be my Rock; and let the God of my salvation be exalted."

While I pray that Your kingdom may come in my own heart, I would especially pray for its extension throughout the world. Arise, O God, and let Your enemies be scattered. May the blessed day soon arrive when a rejoicing and emancipated world shall own no longer habitations of darkness and horrid cruelty — when Jew and Gentile shall welcome the Prince of Peace to the Throne of Universal Empire — and "all ends of the earth shall see the salvation of God." "Come, Lord Jesus; come quickly." Let the cry soon break over Your now burdened Church, "Let us be glad and rejoice, for the marriage of the Lamb is come and His wife has made herself ready." Grant, Lord, that *I* may be in readiness to meet You. May my loins now be girded, and my lamp brightly burning, that, at the Bride-groom's summons, I may be able joyfully to respond, "Lo, this is my God! I have waited for Him."

Grant this day to all near and dear to me, as well as to myself, the special tokens of Your blessing and love. Fold my beloved friends in the arms of Your mercy. Teaching them to do Your holy will, say of them and to them, "The same is my mother, and sister, and brother." Guide us all by Your counsel here. May we feel that the way in which You are leading us is the kindest and the best that covenant love can devise; and when our appointed time on earth is finished, receive us into everlasting habitations through Jesus Christ our Lord.

And now, to God the Father, God the Son, and God the Holy Spirit be ascribed, as is most due, all blessing, and honor, and glory, and praise, world without end. Amen.

"Let the morning bring me word of Your unfailing love, for I have put my trust in You. Show me the way I should go, for to You I lift up my soul."

THE NIGHT WATCHES

Content

1st Evening
THE GLORY OF GOD — 77
2nd Evening
THE IMMUTABILITY OF GOD — 79
3rd Evening
THE OMNIPOTENCE OF GOD — 81
4th Evening
THE OMNIPRESENCE OF GOD — 83
5th Evening
THE WISDOM OF GOD — 85
6th Evening
THE HOLINESS OF GOD — 87
7th Evening
THE JUSTICE OF GOD — 89
8th Evening
THE LOVE OF GOD — 91
9th Evening
THE GRACE OF GOD — 93
10th Evening
THE TENDERNESS OF GOD — 95
11th Evening
THE PATIENCE OF GOD — 97
12th Evening
THE FAITHFULNESS OF GOD — 99
13th Evening
THE SOVEREIGNTY OF GOD — 101
14th Evening
THE PROVIDENCE OF GOD — 103
15th Evening
THE WORD OF GOD — 105
16th Evening
THE SPIRIT OF GOD — 107

17th Evening
THE PROMISES OF GOD   109

18th Evening
THE WARNINGS OF GOD   111

19th Evening
THE CHASTISEMENTS OF GOD   113

20th Evening
THE INVITATIONS OF GOD   115

21st Evening
THE CONSOLATIONS OF GOD   117

22nd Evening
THE PATHS OF GOD   119

23rd Evening
THE SECRET OF GOD   121

24th Evening
THE NAME OF GOD   123

25th Evening
THE FAVOR OF GOD   125

26th Evening
THE JEWELS OF GOD   127

27th Evening
THE JUDGMENT OF GOD   129

28th Evening
GOD'S BANQUETING HOUSE   131

29th Evening
THE PRESENCE OF GOD   133

30th Evening
THE PATH OF DUTY   135

31st Evening
GOD'S CLOSING CALL   137

"I remember You upon my bed — and meditate on You in the *night watches*." — Psalm 63:6

"My soul waits for the Lord more than those who watch for the morning." — Psalm 130:6

"Yet the Lord will command His loving-kindness in the day time, and in the *night* His song shall be with me, and my prayer unto the God of my life." — Psalm 42:8

1st Evening
THE GLORY OF GOD

"Before the mountains were born or You brought forth the earth and the world, even from everlasting to everlasting, you are God!" — Psalm 90:2

O My Soul! Seek to fill yourself with thoughts of the Almighty. Lose yourself in the impenetrable tracts of His Glory!

"Can you by searching find out God?" Can the *insect* fathom the ocean, or the *worm* scale the skies? Can the *finite* comprehend the Infinite? Can the *mortal* grasp Immortality? We can do no more than stand on the brink of the shoreless sea, and cry, "Oh the depth!"

"From everlasting!" — shrouded in the great and amazing mystery of eternity! Before one star revolved in its sphere — before one angel moved his wing — God was! His own infinite presence filling all *space*. All *time*, to Him, is but as the heaving of a breath — the beat of a pulse — the twinkling of an eye!

The Eternity of bliss, which is the noblest heritage of the creature, is in its nature progressive. It admits of advance in degrees of happiness and glory. Not so the Eternity of the Great Creator; He was as *perfect* before the *birth of time* — as He will be when "time shall be no longer!" He was as infinitely *glorious* when He inhabited the solitudes of immensity alone — as He is now with the songs of angel and archangel sounding in His ear! But "who can show forth all His praise?" We can at best but lisp the *alphabet* of His glory. Moses, who saw more of God than most, makes it still his prayer, "I beseech You, show me Your glory!" Paul, who knew more of God than other men, prays still, "that I may *know* Him." "Our safest *eloquence* concerning Him," says Hooker, "is our *silence*, when we confess that His glory is inexplicable."

And is this the Being to whom I can look up with sweetest confidence — and call "My Father"? Is it this Infinite One, whom "the Heaven of Heavens cannot contain," I can call "My God"?

Believer, contemplate the medium through which it is you can see the glory of God, and yet live. "No man has seen God at any time, the only-begotten Son, who is in the bosom of the Father, He has revealed Him." He who dwells in inaccessible light, comes forth from the *pavilion of His glory* in the person of "Immanuel, God with us." In Christ, "the Image of the invisible God," the creature — yes, sinners — can gaze unconsumed on the lusters of Deity! Be it yours to glorify Him. Seek thus to fulfill the great design of your being. Let all your words and ways, your actions and purposes, your crosses and losses, redound to His praise. The highest seraph can have no higher or nobler end than this — the glory of the God before whom he casts his crown.

But He has a claim on you, which He has not on the unredeemed angels. "He gave Himself for you!" This mightiest of all boons which Omnipotence could give, is the guarantee for the bestowment of all lesser necessary blessings, and for the withholding of all unnecessary trials. While you are called to behold "His glory, the glory as of the only-begotten of the Father," remember its characteristic; it is not a glory to appall you by its *splendors* — but to win and captivate you by its *beauties* — it is "full of grace and truth." He is your God in covenant. "Underneath are the everlasting arms." You may compose yourself on your nightly pillow, with the sweet pledge of security, and say, "I will both lie down and sleep in peace, for You alone, O Lord, make me live in safety!" — Psalm 4:8

2nd Evening
THE IMMUTABILITY OF GOD

"But You are the same — and Your years will never end." — Psalm 102:27

What a *fountain of comfort* is to be found in the *Immutability* of God! Not one ripple can disturb the calm of His unchanging nature. Were it so, He would no longer be a perfect Being — He would un-deify Himself — He would cease to be God!

Change is our portion here on earth. "They shall perish!" is the brief chronicle regarding everything on this side Heaven. The *skies* above us, the *earth* beneath us, the *elements* around us shall be destroyed. "All the stars of the heavens will be dissolved and the sky rolled up like a scroll! The stars will fall from the sky like withered leaves from a grapevine, or shriveled figs from a fig tree!" Isaiah 34:4

Scenes of hallowed endearment — they have fled! *Friends* who sweetened our pilgrimage with their presence — they are gone! But here is a sure and safe anchorage amid the world's heaving ocean of vicissitude: "But You are the same — and Your years will never end." All is changing — but the Unchanging One! The earthly scaffolding may give way — but the living Temple remains. The reed may bend to the blast — but the living Rock spurns and outlives the storm!

How blessed, especially, to contemplate the unchangeableness of our *Great High Priest*, "Jesus Christ, the same yesterday, and today, and forever!" True, He is, in one sense, "changed." No longer the *Man of sorrows*; no longer the *homeless wanderer*. He is *enthroned* amid the glories of Heaven. Seraphs praise Him — Saints adore Him. But His Heart knows no change. His ascension glories have not obliterated His tender human sympathies. We can think of Him receiving an outcast sinner, or stilling the storm, or standing at the gate of Nain, or weeping tears of pity over a lost city, or tears of sympathy over a buried friend — and write over all these, "You are the same!" The name which He bequeathed by angels to His Church until He comes again is, "that *same* Jesus!" His own Patmos title is His memorial for all time, "I AM He who lives!"

Believer! has He ever seemed to change towards you? Are you

even now mourning over the withdrawal of that countenance whose smile is heaven? Are you saying in the bitterness of your spirit, "Has the Lord forgotten to be gracious?" The change is with yourself — and not with your God. Behind the *clouds* of your own departure, the *Sun* of His love shines brightly as ever. "He faints not, neither is weary."

Or, it may be, you are laboring under severe trials. The hand of your God may be heavy upon you. The secret thought may be harbored that some *tear* might have been spared; that your *chastisement* might have been less severe — that your *bereavement*, with its dark accompaniment, might have been mitigated or averted. Look *upwards* and take the Psalmist's antidote as your own, "I will remember the years of the right hand of the Most High God." Think that the same Hand which for you was nailed to the Cross — is now pleading for you on the Throne; ordering and controlling every trial; and over every dark providence writing the unanswerable challenge, "He who spared not His own Son — but delivered Him up for us all, how shall He not with Him also freely give us all things?"

Oh! thus pillowing your head on the Immutability of Jesus, amid the crude buffetings of a changing world, you will be able to say — until the dawn of the morning breaks on you, which knows neither night nor vicissitude, "I will both lie down and sleep in peace, for You alone, O Lord, make me live in safety!" — Psalm 4:8

3rd Evening
THE OMNIPOTENCE OF GOD

"The Lord God omnipotent reigns!" — Revelation 19:6

Believer! what can better support and sustain you amid the trials of your pilgrimage, than the thought that you have an Omnipotent arm to lean upon? The God with whom you have to do — is boundless in His resources! There is no *crossing* His designs — no *thwarting* His purposes — no *questioning* His counsels. His mandate is law! "He speaks — and it is done!" Your need is great. From the humblest crumb of providential goodness, up to the richest blessing of Divine grace — you are hanging from moment to moment, as a poor pensioner on Jehovah's bounty! But, fear not! "I am the Almighty God!" Finite necessities can never exhaust My infinite fullness! "My God will supply all your needs according to His glorious riches in Christ Jesus!"

To You, O blessed Jesus! *all power* has been committed in Heaven and in earth. "ALL power!" He has in His hands the reigns of universal empire! To "the Lion of the tribe of Judah" has been entrusted the seven-sealed scroll of Providence. Whatever is the blessing which the poorest, weakest, loneliest, most afflicted of His saints require — if it is really for their good — the "Wonderful Counselor" secures it. "As a Prince, He has power with God," and must "prevail."

He combines in His adorable Person, all that a sinner requires: a Heart tender enough to love; and a Hand strong enough to save. The Elder Brother! the "Mighty God!" How He delights in the exercise of His omnipotence in behalf of His own people — in ruling over their interests, and overruling their trials for their eternal good! When He prays for *Himself*, it is "Not *My* will." When He prays for *them*, it is, "Father, *I* will!" I may well take the *motto* which He still bears on His breastplate before the Throne, as the ground of support and encouragement in all time of tribulation, "able to save to the uttermost!"

My *enemies* are many — their name is Legion:

Satan, the great adversary;
heart traitors — bosom sins;

the *world*, and the world's trinity: "the lusts of the flesh, and the lusts of the eye, and the pride of life!"

But He who is *for* me, is greater far than all that can be *against* me. He is "stronger" than the "strong man." "Christ the Power of God." "I, who speak in righteousness, am mighty to save!"

Believer, are you in trial, beaten down with a great fight of afflictions — like the disciples, out in a midnight of storm, buffeting a sea of trouble? Fear not! When the *tempest* has done its work, when the *trial* has fulfilled its mission — the voice which hushed the waters of old, has only to give forth the omnipotent mandate, *"Peace, be still!"* and immediately there will be a great calm! The "all power" of Jesus! — what a pillow on which to rest my aching head; disarming all my fears, and inducing thoughts of sweetest comfort, consolation, and joy! "I will both lie down and sleep in peace, for You alone, O Lord, make me live in safety!" — Psalm 4:8

4th Evening
THE OMNIPRESENCE OF GOD

"Where shall I go from Your Spirit? Where shall I flee from Your presence?" — Psalm 139:7

The omnipresence of God! How baffling to any finite comprehension! To think that *above* us, and *around* us, and *within* us — there is Deity — the invisible footprints of an Omniscient, Omnipresent One! "His Eyes are in every place;" on rolling planets — and tiny atoms; on the bright seraph — and the lowly worm; roaming in searching scrutiny through the tracks of immensity — and reading the dark and hidden page of my heart! "All things are naked and opened unto the eyes of Him with whom we have to do!"

O God! shall this Your Omnipresence appall me? No! In my seasons of *sadness* and *sorrow* and *loneliness* — when other comforts and comforters have failed — when, it may be, in the darkness and silence of some midnight hour, in vain I have sought repose — how sweet to think, "My God is here! I am not alone. The Omniscient One, to whom the darkness and the light are both alike — is hovering over my sleepless pillow!" "He who keeps Israel neither slumbers nor sleeps!" O my *Unsetting Sun*, it cannot be darkness or loneliness or sadness — where You are. There can be no *night* to the soul which has been cheered with Your glorious radiance!

"Surely, I am with you always!" How precious, blessed Jesus, is this Your legacy of parting love! Present with each of Your people until the end of time — ever present, omnipresent. The true "Pillar of cloud" by day and "Pillar of fire" by night, preceding and encamping by us in every step of our wilderness journey. My soul! think of Him, at this moment, in the mysteriousness of His Godhead nature — and yet, with all the exquisitely tender sympathies of a glorified Humanity — as present with every member of the family that He has redeemed with His blood! Yes, and as much present with every individual soul, as if He had none other to care for — but as if that one engrossed all His affection and love!

The Great *Builder* — surveying every stone and pillar of His spiritual temple; the Great *Shepherd* — with His eye on every sheep of His fold; the Great *High Priest* — marking every tear-drop; noting every sorrow; listening to every prayer; knowing the peculiarities of every case; no number perplexing Him — no variety bewildering Him; able to *attend* to all, and *satisfy* all, and *answer* all — myriads drawing hourly from His Treasury — and yet no diminution of that Treasury — ever emptying, and yet ever filling, and always full!

Jesus! Your perpetual and all-pervading presence turns darkness into day! I am not left un-befriended to weather the storms of life — Your hand is from hour to hour piloting my frail vessel. The omnipresence of God--*gracious antidote to every earthly sorrow!*

«I have set the Lord always before me!» Even now, as night is drawing its curtains around me, be this my closing prayer, ‹Blessed Savior! abide with me, for it is toward evening, and the day is far spent!' Under the shadowing wings of Your presence and love, «I will both lie down and sleep in peace, for You alone, O Lord, make me live in safety!» — Psalm 4:8

5th Evening
THE WISDOM OF GOD

"His understanding is infinite!" —Psalm 147:5

How baffling often are God's dispensations! The more we attempt to fathom their mystery — the more we are driven to rest in the best earthly solution, "Your judgments are a great deep!" But where sense says, *"All these things are against me!"* — faith has a different verdict, *"All things are working together for my good!"* This is the province of faith, confidingly to lean on the arm of God, and to say, "The Lord is righteous in all His ways."

We speak of God "foreseeing," but the past, present, and future — are with Him all alike. He sees the end from the beginning. We can discern but a short way, and that, through an imperfect and distorted medium. In a piece of earthly mechanism we seldom can discover beauty in the uncompleted structure. The mightiest works of science, while in progress — often appear a chaos of confusion. It is only when finished that we can admire the relation and adjustment of every part to the whole. So also with the mechanism of God's moral administration. At present, how much mystery! But, when in the light of eternity we come to contemplate the completion of the mighty plan, how shall we be brought to own and exclaim, "The works of the Lord are right!"

Believer, are the dealings of your God at present displaying a mysterious aspect to you? Are you about to enter some dark cloud, exclaiming, "Truly, You are a God that hides Yourself?" Do you "fear to enter the cloud?" Take courage! It will be with you as with the disciples on their Mount of Transfiguration; unexpected glimpses of heavenly glory — unlooked-for tokens of the Savior's presence and love await you! If your Lord leads you into the *cloud* — follow Him. If He "constrains you to get into the ship," — obey Him. The *cloud* will burst in blessings. The ship will conduct you (it may be over a stormy sea) to a quiet haven at last. It is only the *surface* of the ocean that is rough. All beneath is a deep calm; and in every threatening wave there is a "needs-be!"

Oh! trust Him, who is emphatically "The Wisdom of God." He is your Counselor — combining the infinite knowledge of God with the experience and sympathy of man. He is pledged to use the discipline most wisely suited for each believer's case.

Under the blessed persuasion, that a day of disclosures is at hand, when, "in Your light, I shall see light," I will trust the divine wisdom which I cannot fathom; and repeat, as the shadows of evening gather around me, until the night of earth's ignorance vanishes before the breaking of an eternal day, "I will both lie down and sleep in peace, for You alone, O Lord, make me live in safety!" — Psalm 4:8

6th Evening
THE HOLINESS OF GOD

"You only are holy!" — Revelation 15:4

What a sublime perfection is this! It would seem to form the loftiest theme for the adorations of saints and angels. They cease not day nor night to cry, "Holy, Holy, Holy, Lord God Almighty!" It evokes from the Church on earth her loudest strains, "Let them praise His great and awesome name, for it is Holy!"

Reader, seek, in some feeble measure, to apprehend the nature of God's unswerving hatred at sin! It is the deep, deliberate, innate holiness of His nature which requires Him to hate moral evil, and to visit it with impartial punishment.

But what pleasure can there be in meditating on so solemn a theme? The contemplation of a God "of purer eyes than to behold iniquity" — in whose sight "the heavens are not clean!" Jesus! Your glorious *atonement* is the mirror in which we can gaze un-appalled on this august attribute! Your *cross* is, to the wide universe, a perpetual monument and memorial of the Holiness of God. It proclaims, as nothing else could, "You love righteousness — and hate wickedness!" Through that cross, the Holiest of all Beings becomes the most gracious of all. "Now, we can love Him," says a saint who has entered on his rest, "not only *although* He is holy — but *because* He is holy."

Gaze, and gaze again on that monumental cross, until it teaches the lesson! How vain elsewhere to look for pardon; how delusive that dream on which multitudes peril their eternal safety, that God will be at last *too merciful* to punish! Surely, if any less solemn vindication could have sufficed — or had it been compatible with the rectitude of the Divine nature, and the requirements of the Divine law, to dispense pardon in any other way — then Gethsemane and Calvary, with all their awful exponents of agony, would have been spared. The *Almighty victim* would not have voluntarily submitted to a life of ignominy and a death of woe — if, by any simpler method, He could have "cleared the guilty." But this was impossible. If He was to "save others," He could not save Himself!

Believer, seek that some faint and feeble emanations from this Divine attribute of Holiness may be yours. Let *"Holiness to the*

Lord" be the superscription on your *heart* and *life*. Abounding grace can give no sanction or encouragement to abound in sin. 'His mercy,' says Reynolds, 'is a holy mercy which knows how to pardon sin — not to protect it; it is a sanctuary for the penitent — not for the presumptuous.'

Oh, are you tempted to murmur under the dealings of your God? What are the sorest of your trials — in comparison with what they might have been, had this Holy God left you to know, in all the sternness of its meaning, how "Glorious He is in Holiness"? Rather marvel, considering your sins, that your *trial* has been so small — your *cross* so light. Blessed Jesus! into this sanctuary of "holy mercy" which You have opened for me — I will flee. I can now "give thanks at the remembrance of God's holiness." Deriving, even from this splendid attribute, one of the 'songs in the night', "I will both lie down and sleep in peace, for You alone, O Lord, make me live in safety!" — Psalm 4:8

7th Evening
THE JUSTICE OF GOD

"Righteousness and justice are the habitation of Your throne!"
— Psalm 89:14

The *Justice* of God is "His Holiness in exercise." Let us go to the spot marked out as the scene of its most solemn manifestation. In the depths of eternity past, the summons was heard, "Awake, O Sword, against My Shepherd, and against the Man who is My Fellow!" That mysterious commission has been fulfilled. The Shepherd has been smitten. Myriads of condemned spirits could not have borne God's inexorable rectitude as when, on the cross of Calvary, One lone voice sent up the wailing cry, *"My God, My God, why have You forsaken Me!"*

Believer, rejoice! *Justice*, which before had demanded the execution of a righteous doom upon lost millions — can now unite with *Mercy* in sheathing the avenging sword and exulting over redeemed myriads. The *Law* which brought in a whole world "guilty before God," can exult with Mercy — in seeing its every requirement obeyed, its every demand fulfilled; the Lawgiver Himself "the Just and yet the Justifier;" unloosing every chain of condemnation, and pronouncing "Not guilty!" "O Law!" says Luther, "I drown my conscience in the wounds, blood, death, resurrection, and victory of Christ!"

Wondrous thought! — Justice, the very attribute which *excluded* the sinner — has become the first to throw open a door of welcome; proclaiming that infinite merit — has cancelled infinite demerit; infinite holiness — has covered infinite sin! While "righteousness and justice" are the habitation of God's throne, provision has been made whereby, in perfect consistency with every principle of His moral government, "mercy and truth" may go continually before His face!

Reader, it is well for you often to thus devoutly dwell on the *inflexible Justice* of your God. It will magnify and enhance to you, the riches of His grace, the glories of redemption, and the preciousness of Jesus. If the sinner is to be saved, "judgment must be laid to the line, and righteousness to the plummet!" Says Lefevre, "The Sinless One must be condemned — if he who is guilty is to go free. The Blessed One must bear the curse — if the cursed ones are to be brought into blessing. The Life must die — if the dead are to live!" "In prayer one evening," says Henry Martyn, "I had such near and frightening views of God's judgment upon sinners in Hell, that my flesh trembled for fear of them. I flew trembling to Jesus Christ, as if the flames were taking hold of me! Oh! Christ will indeed save me — or else I must perish!"

My soul! take hold of that touchingly simple assurance to which Justice has appended its seal, "Whoever believes in Him shall not perish!" "Not perish!" Justice, and a God of justice, proclaiming so great salvation — safety from the terrors of a violated law — rest from the accusations of a guilty conscience — calmness in the prospect of death! Grace here! Glory hereafter! Oh, what more can the sinner need — or God bestow! "I will both lie down and sleep in peace, for You alone, O Lord, make me live in safety!" — Psalm 4:8

8th Evening
THE LOVE OF GOD

"God is love." — 1 John 4:16

"The only real mystery of the Bible," says an old writer, "is a mystery of Love." "God so loved the world — that He gave His only begotten Son." What? For a lost and ruined world — the Prince of Life should leave His Throne of glory, travel down to a valley of tears, and expire by an ignominious death on the bitter tree! Love unutterable! Love unspeakable! The reflection of the skeptic of a by-gone age, may have formed at times the musing of better minds, "This is far too great — it is far too good to be true!" Infinite majesty — compassionating infinite weakness! The great Sun of heaven, the Fountain of uncreated light — undergoing an eclipse of darkness and blood for the sake of a candle that glimmered in nothingness, in comparison with His beams.

"God so loved the world!" Man never can get farther in the solution of the wondrous problem. Eternity itself will form a ladder — the saints climbing step by step its ascending glories — but, as the prospect widens, each will elicit the same confession, "The love of Christ, which surpasses knowledge!"

My soul! seek to enter into the secrets of this Love of your adorable Redeemer! Before all time — that love began. We have glimpses of it bursting out from the recesses of a past eternity, "Then I was by Him, as one brought up with Him, and I was daily His delight, rejoicing always before Him!" And "when the fullness of the time had come," though He foresaw all His untold sufferings — nothing would deter Him from pursuing His anguished path, "He set His face steadfastly to go to Jerusalem." More — as if *longing* for the hour of victory, He exclaimed, "There is a terrible baptism ahead of Me — and I am under a heavy burden until it is accomplished!"

Think of that love now! The *live coals*, in the censer of old, form a feeble type of the burning ardor of affection still manifested by our Great High Priest within the veil, in behalf of His own people. There He bears the name of each of them, indelibly engraved on His breastplate. Loving them at the beginning — He will love them even unto the end. Earthly love may grow cold and changeable; earthly love may die. Not so the love of this "Friend of friends." His love is as strong as death — surviving death — no, as deathless as eternity! Listen to His own exponent of its intensity, "As the Father has loved Me — so have I loved you!" "You see in Him;" says an old writer, "an ocean of love without bottom, without bounds, overflowing the banks of Heaven, streaming down to this world to wash away the vileness of man!"

Blessed Jesus! how cold, and fitful, and transient has been *my* love to You — in comparison of *Your* love to me! Bring me more under its constraining influence. May this be the superscription on all my thoughts and actions — on all my occupations and my time, 'I am not my own. Lord, I am Yours! How can I love You enough, Who so loves me! My life shall henceforth be one thank-offering of praise for Your redeeming mercies!'

Standing this night on the shores of this illimitable ocean — surveying its length and breadth — every wave murmuring, "Peace on earth — and good-will to men," "I will both lie down and sleep in peace, for You alone, O Lord, make me live in safety!" — Psalm 4:8

9th Evening
THE GRACE OF GOD

"The God of all grace." — 1 Peter 5:10

"By the Grace of God — I am what I am!" This is the believer's eternal confession. Grace found him a *rebel* against God — it leaves him a *son* of God! Grace found him wandering at the gates of Hell — it leaves him at the gates of Heaven! Grace devised the scheme of Redemption. Justice never would; Reason never could. And it is Grace which carries out that scheme. No sinner would ever have sought God — but "by grace." The thickets of Eden would have proved *Adam's* grave — had not grace called him out. *Saul* would have lived and died the haughty self-righteous persecutor — had not grace laid him low. The *thief on the cross* would have continued breathing out his blasphemies — had not grace arrested his tongue and tuned it for glory. "Out of the *knottiest timber*," says Rutherford, "God can make *vessels of mercy* for service in the high palace of glory!"

"I came, I saw, I conquered!" may be inscribed by the Savior on every *monument of His grace.* "I *came* to the sinner; I *looked* upon him; and with a look of omnipotent love — I *conquered* him!"

Believer, you would have been this day a wandering star, to whom is reserved the blackness of darkness forever! You would have been Christless — hopeless — portionless; had not grace invited you, and grace constrained you! And it is grace which, at this moment, "keeps" you. You have often been a *Peter* — forsaking your Lord — but brought back to Him again. Why have you not been a *Demas* or a *Judas?* "I have prayed for you — that your faith fail not." Is not this your own comment and reflection on life's retrospect: "Yet not I — but the grace of God which was with me!"

Seek to realize your dependence on this grace every moment. *"More grace! more grace!"* needs to be your continual cry. His infinite *supply* — is commensurate with your infinite *need.* The treasury of grace, though always emptying — is always full. The *key of prayer* which opens it — is always at hand! And the *Almighty Bestower* of the blessings of grace — is always "waiting to be gracious." The recorded promise can never be cancelled or reversed, "My grace is sufficient for you."

Reader! seek to dwell much on this inexhaustible theme! The grace of God is the source of lesser *temporal* blessings — as well as of higher *spiritual* blessings. Grace accounts for the *crumb of daily bread* — as well as for the *crown of eternal glory!* But even in regard to earthly mercies, never forget the CHANNEL of grace: *"through Christ Jesus!"* It is sweet thus to connect every blessing, even the smallest and humblest token of providential bounty — with Calvary's cross — to have the common blessings of life stamped with "the print of the nails!" It makes them doubly precious to think, *"All this flows from Jesus!"*

Let others be contented with the un-covenanted mercies of God. Be it mine to say, as the child of grace, and heir of glory — 'My Father in Heaven, give me today my daily bread.' Reposing in the "all sufficiency in all things" promised by "the God of all grace," "I will both lie down and sleep in peace, for You alone, O Lord, make me live in safety!" — Psalm 4:8

10th Evening
THE TENDERNESS OF GOD

"He will feed his flock like a shepherd. He will carry the lambs in His arms, holding them close to His heart. He will gently lead the mother sheep with their young." — Isaiah 40:11

How soothing, in the hour of sorrow, or bereavement, or death — to have the countenance and sympathy of a tender earthly friend. Reader, these words tell you of One nearer, dearer, and tenderer still — the Friend that never fails — a tender God! By how many endearing epithets does Jesus exhibit the tenderness of His relation to His people. Does a *shepherd* watch tenderly over his flock? "The Lord is my Shepherd." Does a *father* exercise fondest solicitude towards his children? "I will be a Father unto you." Does a *mother's love* exceed all other earthly types of affection. "As one whom his mother comforts — so will I comfort you." Is the 'apple of the eye' (the pupil) the most sensitive part of the most delicate bodily organ? He guards His people "as the apple of His eye!"

When the Shepherd and Guardian of Souls finds the redeemed sinner, like a lost sheep, stumbling on the dark mountains — how tenderly He deals with him! There is no look of wrath — no word of upbraiding; in silent love "He lays him on His shoulders rejoicing!"

When *Peter* fell, Jesus did not unnecessarily wound him. He might have repeated often and again, the *piercing look* which brought the flood of penitential sorrow. But He gave that look only once; and when He reminded Peter of his threefold denial, it was by thrice repeating the gentlest of questions, *"Do you love Me?"*

Reader, are you mourning over the weakness of your faith; the coldness of your love; your manifold spiritual declensions? Fear not! He knows your frame! He will give 'feeble faith' *tender dealing*. He will "carry" in His arms those that are unable to walk, and will conduct the burdened ones through a path less rough and rugged than others.

When "the lion" or "the bear" comes, you may trust the *true David*, the tenderest of Shepherds! Are you suffering from outward trial? Confide in the tenderness of your God's dealings with you. The strokes of His *rod* are gentle strokes — the *needed discipline* of a father yearning over his children, at the very moment he is chastising them. The gentlest earthly parent may speak a harsh word at times; it may be needlessly harsh. But not so with God. He may seem, like *Joseph* to his brethren, to speak roughly; but all the while there is *love in His heart.*

The 'pruning knife' will not be used unnecessarily — it will never cut too deeply! The 'furnace' will not burn more fiercely than is absolutely required — a tender God is seated by it, tempering the fury of its flames!

And what, believer, is the secret of all this tenderness? "There is a Man upon the Throne!" Jesus, the God-Man Mediator; combining with the might of *Godhead* — the tenderness of *spotless humanity.* Is your heart crushed with sorrow? So was His! Are your eyes dimmed with tears? So were His! "Jesus wept!" *Bethany's Chief Mourner* still wears the *Brother's heart* in glory. Others may be unable to enter into the depths of your trial — He can — He does!

With such a "tender God" caring for me, providing for me, watching my path by day, and guarding my couch by night, "I will both lie down and sleep in peace, for You alone, O Lord, make me live in safety!" — Psalm 4:8

11th Evening
THE PATIENCE OF GOD

"The God of patience." — Romans 15:5

There is no more wondrous subject than this — "The Patience of God." Think of the lapse of *ages* during which that patience has lasted 6,000 years! Think of the *multitudes* who have been the subjects of it — millions on millions, in successive climates and centuries! Think of the *sins* which have, all that time, been trying and wearying that patience — their number — their heinousness — their aggravation! The world's history is a consecutive *history of iniquity* — a lengthened provocation of the Almighty's forbearance! The Church, like a feeble ark, tossed on a mighty ocean of unbelief; and yet the world, with its cumberers, still spared! The cry of its sinful millions at this moment enters "the ears of the Lord Almighty" and yet, "for all this," His hand of mercy is "stretched out still!"

And *who* is this God of patience? It is the Almighty Being who could strike these millions down in a moment; who could, by a breath, annihilate the world — no, who would require no positive or visible putting forth of His omnipotence to effect this — but simply to *withdraw His sustaining arm!*

Surely, of all the examples of the Almighty's power, there is none more wondrous or amazing than "God's power over Himself." He is "slow to anger." "Judgment is His strange work." He "shows mercy unto thousands." God bears for 1500 years, from Moses to Jesus, with *Israel's* unbelief; and yet, as a writer remarks, "He speaks of it as but *a day.*" "All *day* long have I stretched out My hands to a disobedient and obstinate people." What explanation for this tenderness? "My thoughts are not your thoughts, neither are your ways My ways — says the Lord!"

Believer, how great has been God's patience towards you! In your unconverted state, when a wanderer from His fold, with what unwearied love He went after you; notwithstanding all your waywardness; never ceasing the pursuit "until He found you!" Think of your fainting and weariness since being converted — your ever-changing frames and feelings — the ebbings and the flowings in the tide of your love; and yet, instead of surrendering you to your own perverse will, His language concerning you is, "How can I give you up?" For a lifetime, your Savior-God has been standing knocking at your door; and His attitude is still the same, "Behold, I stand!"

How should the patience of Jesus lead me to be submissive under trial! When He has so long borne with me, shall not I "bear" with Him? When I think of His patience under a far heavier cross, can I murmur — when He murmured not! No, I will check every repining thought, and looking up, in confiding affection, to "the God of all patience," "I will both lie down and sleep in peace, for You alone, O Lord, make me live in safety!" — Psalm 4:8

12th Evening
THE FAITHFULNESS OF GOD

"Your mercy, O LORD, is in the heavens; and your faithfulness reaches unto the clouds." — Psalm 36:5

It has been well said, that "the universe is a parable of grace." "Just as the mountains surround and protect Jerusalem, so the Lord surrounds and protects His people, both now and forever." But more stable than even these types of immutability in the kingdom of nature, is the word of a Covenant-keeping God in the kingdom of grace. These mountains (nature's best emblems of steadfastness) may depart, and the hills be removed, "but," says their Almighty Maker, "My kindness shall not be taken from you!" We can look upwards to the stars of night, and see the "faithfulness" of God "established" in the material heavens, "They continue, to this day, according to Your plans; for all are Your servants." But these are feeble types and symbols of brighter constellations in the spiritual skies — the declarations of an unchanging God, "Your Word is forever settled in Heaven!"

What a gracious assurance amid our own unfaithfulness, "The Lord is faithful!" My soul, anchor yourself on this rock of the Divine veracity. Take hold of that blessed parenthesis which has been, to many a tossed soul, as a polar star in its nights of darkness, "Having loved His own who were in the world — He loved them unto the end." He loves them in life — loves them in death — loves them through death — loves them into glory!

Are you not at this hour — a *monument of God's faithfulness?* Where would you have been, had not the *magnet of His grace* kept you, and drawn your fugitive affections towards Himself? From how many temptations He has rescued you — laying hold of you on the precipice, when about to plunge headlong down; employing, sometimes *constraining* grace, at other times, *restraining* grace — making this your brief history: "Kept by the power of God!" and overruling all — ALL for His own glory, and your own good!

I love to think of Your faithfulness, O "Tried stone — laid in Zion." You were tried by the Law — by Justice — by the fierce assaults and temptations of Satan — by the mockings and revilings and cruelties of wicked men; and yet You remain faithful! You have been tried in another sense by Prophets and Apostles; by Martyrs and Saints; by youthful sinners, and aged sinners, and dying sinners — and You have been found "faithful," by all and to all; and You are faithful still!

Reader, never suppose, amid the unfaithfulness of earth's trusted friends, that you are doomed to thread your way in loneliness and solitude. There is more than one 'Emmaus journey.' The "abiding" Friend is still here! He is always the same. "He faints not, neither is weary!" His *faithfulness* is a tried faithfulness. His *Word* is a tried Word. His *friendship* is a tried friendship. He is always *better* than His Word. He pays 'with interest'!

When I think that at this very moment the eye of that faithful Savior God is upon me, "I will both lie down and sleep in peace, for You alone, O Lord, make me live in safety!" — Psalm 4:8

13th Evening
THE SOVEREIGNTY OF GOD

"All the peoples of the earth are regarded as nothing. He does as He pleases with the powers of heaven and the peoples of the earth. No one can hold back His hand or say to Him: What have You done?" — Daniel 4:35

How blessed that elementary truth, "The Lord reigns!" To know that there is no *chance* or *accident* with God — that He decrees the fall of a sparrow — the destruction of a speck — the annihilation of a world!

The Almighty is not like Baal, "asleep." "He who keeps Israel" can never for a moment "slumber." *Man proposes — but God disposes!* "God has done it!" is the history of every event, past, present, and to come. His *purposes* — none can change; His *counsels* — none can resist.

Believer, how cheering to know that all that befalls you, is thus ordered in the eternal purpose of a Covenant God! Every minute circumstance of your lot — appointing the bounds of your habitation — meting out *every drop* in the cup of life — arranging what by you is called its "vicissitudes" — decreeing all its trials; and at last, as the great Proprietor of life, revoking the lease of existence when its allotted term has expired!

How it should keep the mind from its guilty proneness to brood and fret over second causes, were this grand but simple truth ever realized — that all that befalls us are integral parts in a stupendous plan of wisdom — that there is no crossing or thwarting the designs and dealings of God! None can say, "What have You done?" All ought to say, "He has done all things well."

We dare not venture, with presumptuous gaze, to penetrate into "those secret things which belong unto the Lord our God." In all that is fitting, in the consideration of this august theme of the Divine Decrees, to impart encouragement and consolation, let us rejoice. In all that is mysterious and incomprehensible, let us with childlike reverence exclaim, "Oh, what a wonderful God we have! How great are His riches and wisdom and knowledge! How impossible it is for us to understand His decisions and His methods! For who can know what the Lord is thinking? Who knows enough to be His counselor? And who could ever give Him so much that He would have to pay it back? For everything comes from Him; everything exists by His power and is intended for His glory. To Him be glory evermore. Amen!"

The contemplation of the Sovereignty of God formed subject-matter of rejoicing to the Savior Himself in His humiliation, "Even so, Father, for so it seemed good in Your sight!" What supplied material for comfort and joy to an Almighty Sufferer — may well dry the tears and soothe the pangs of His suffering people! Oh, how sinners may magnify their God by a calm submission to His will; by seeing no hand but One in their trials; in giving — or taking: "Naked I came from my mother's womb, and naked I will depart. The Lord *gave* — and the Lord has taken away; may the name of the Lord be praised!" "Which of all these does not know that the hand of the Lord has done this?"

Will it not further help to the breathing of the prayer, "May Your will be done," when I think, in connection with the Sovereignty of God, of the grand end of His immutable decrees — it is, "His own glory." "Of Him, and through Him, and to Him, are *all things*." What more can I desire? "All things." — God's glory and my own good! "I will both lie down and sleep in peace, for You alone, O Lord, make me live in safety!" — Psalm 4:8

14th Evening
THE PROVIDENCE OF GOD

"His kingdom rules over all." — Psalm 103:19

Believer, try to see God in everything — and everything in God! Lose your own will in His. Enter on no pursuit, engage in no plan, without Paul's prayer and condition, "May the will of the Lord be done." How it would hallow prosperity, and sweeten adversity, thus, in all things, to follow, like Israel, the Guiding Pillar — at His bidding to pitch our tents; at His bidding to depart. Each providence has a *voice* — if we would only hear it. It is a *signpost* in the journey, pointing us to "the right way," that we may go to "the city of habitation."

Often what a mysterious volume *Providence* is! Its every page full of dark hieroglyphics, to which human reason can furnish no key. But faith falls back on the assurance that "the Judge of all the earth must do right." The Father of all His people cannot do wrong. To the common observer, the stars in the nightly heavens are all confused masses, pursuing diverse and erratic courses. But to the astronomer, each has its allotted and prescribed pathway, and all are preserving inviolately, one universal law of harmony and order. It is faith's loftiest prerogative, patiently to wait until 'that day of disclosures,' when page by page the *mysterious book* will be unraveled, and the believer himself will endorse every page with, *"It is well!"*

Providences may even seem to be getting *darker* — merging like declining day into the shadows of twilight. But, contrary to nature, and to the Christian's expectations, "At evening time — it shall be light!" The gathering cloud will then be seen to be fraught only with blessings, which will burst on the believer's head. My soul, be still, and know that He is God! "Rest in the Lord, and wait patiently for Him." The mysterious "why" you have so long been waiting for, will soon be revealed. The long night-watch will soon terminate in the looked-for, longed-for morning.

Blessed Lord! my pilgrimage path is studded thick with *Ebenezers* testifying to Your faithfulness and mercy. I love to think of Your manifold gracious interpositions in the past — God *sustaining* me in trial — God *supporting* me in perplexity — God *rescuing* me when in temptation — God *helping* me when "vain was the help of man!" "When my foot slipped, Your mercy, O Lord, held me up!" And shall I not take all Your goodness previously manifested — as a pledge of faithfulness in the future? In full confidence that You are a "rich Provider," I shall take no anxious thought for the morrow — but repose in this covenant assurance of a covenant-keeping God, "I will never fail you nor forsake you." "I will both lie down and sleep in peace, for You alone, O Lord, make me live in safety!" — Psalm 4:8

15th Evening
THE WORD OF GOD

"Your Word is a lamp unto my feet — and a light unto my path."
— Psalm 119:105

Man's word disappoints — God's Word, never! "The Word of the Lord is tried." It has been tried by the sinner — he neglected it and perished. It has been tried by the saint — he has believed it and has been saved. What a precious *legacy of God* to our world! The volume of NATURE, much as it teaches, is silent on the question of a sinner's acceptance with God. The Scriptures alone can solve the enigma, "How is God to deal with the guilty?" That question unanswered — in peace we could not live, and in peace we dared not die! But glad tidings, O precious messenger from God, have You brought to a doomed earth: "God so loved the world, that He gave His only Son, that whoever believes in Him should not perish — but have everlasting life!" Were there no more in the Divine communication than that one brief entry, the Bible would still be better to us than "millions in gold and silver."

The Word of God is a vast *repository* and *emporium* of heavenly wisdom — free to all — suited for all — intended for all — offered to all. The Word of God is an *inexhaustible mine* — the deeper you dig, the richer the ore. It has a word in season for rich and poor; for young and old; for the *wandering*; for the *doubting*; for the *sorrowing*; for the *believing*; for the *dying*; for the *perishing!*

Reader, sit at the feet of Jesus in His Word, and with the docility of a little child, say, "Speak, Lord — for Your servant is listening!" Always approach it as if it met you with the living salutation, "I have a message from God for you!" There are differences in every heart-chamber — but this *key* fits every door! Make it a faithful *mirror*, in which you see a reflection of yourself! The more faithfully it is held up, the more will the sense of your deficiency and defilement drive you to the atoning blood. In all your difficulties — make it "your counselor." In all your perplexities — make it your *interpreter* and *guide*. In all your sorrows — make it your *fountain of consolation*. In all your *temptations* — make it your ultimate court of appeal. When venturing on debatable ground, let this deter you, "What does the Scripture say?" When assailed, let this protect and defend you, *"It is written!"*

Precious at all times, it is especially precious in "the cloudy and dark day." We may do without our *lamp* in the day; but where are we, without it — in the midnight tempestuous sea? "I would have perished in my affliction," says a sinking cast-away, "but Your Word has quickened me."

Be it mine to look forward to that blessed time, when the intervention of that Word, and all other means of grace, will terminate; for, in Heaven, "they need no *candle*." Meanwhile, pillowing my head on the Word of the eternal God, and with these glorious prospects in view, "I will both lie down and sleep in peace, for You alone, O Lord, make me live in safety!" — Psalm 4:8

16th Evening
THE SPIRIT OF GOD

"Do not take Your Holy Spirit from me." — Psalm 51:11

"It is for your benefit that I go away, because if I do not go away — the Comforter will not come to you. If I go, I will send Him to you." How momentous must be the agency of the Holy Spirit, when the adorable Redeemer represented the Church as being more than compensated for the blank of His own departure — the loss of His own presence — by the gift of this Divine Paraclete!

"It is the Spirit who quickens." It is He who is the Agent in the new birth, "Except a man is born of water, and of the Spirit — he cannot enter into the kingdom of Heaven." It is He who enables the sinner by faith to lay hold on Jesus, and embrace His salvation, "No man can say that Jesus is the Lord — but by the Holy Spirit." It is He who carries on the progressive work of holiness — we are saved "through the *sanctification* of the Spirit." It is He who creates anew the lost image of the Godhead — impresses on the soul the lineaments of the Savior's character, "We are changed into the same image, from glory to glory — by the Lord the Spirit." It is He who illumines the Divine Record, acting like a telescope to the moral vision, unveiling in the *skies of inspiration* "wondrous things" contained in the Word, which the natural eye cannot see. It is He who unfolds the glories of the Redeemer's work — the beauties of His person — the completeness of His sacrifice — the riches of His grace, "He will bring glory to Me by taking from what is Mine — and making it known to you." More — the *soul* of the believer becomes itself a *temple* of the Holy Spirit.

Oh! with what holy jealousy would the child of God guard every avenue to temptation, if this amazing truth exercised its habitual and solemnizing power over him, *"The Spirit of God dwells within me!"* How would he avoid anything and everything by which he would be likely to "grieve" this blessed Agent, "whereby he is sealed until the day of redemption." "Behold!" He seems to say, "I make all things new." The initial operation is His — He broods over the face of the spiritual chaos, saying, "Let there be light!" The closing and consummating grace is His — He conducts the soul through the swellings of Jordan, until it joins with the ransomed multitude before the throne, in ascribing to Father, Son, and Holy Spirit — the glories of a completed salvation!

Take not, then, O God! Your Holy Spirit from me. In vain are the Word, ordinances, sacraments, sermons, prayers — without Him. All are in themselves, passive instruments; His is the omnipotent arm which wields and vanquishes! Our adorable Redeemer — the great High Priest — was Himself *anointed* with the Holy Spirit. That anointing oil, poured upon the Church's living Head, runs down to the skirts of His garment, anointing, as it flows, all His members. And those that are lowest and humblest — nearest the skirts — receive the *most*. Reader, if this is your position — at the feet of Jesus — the blessed influences of the Holy Spirit, streaming down upon you in copious effusion, sanctifying you more and more, and making you more fit for glory — then you may well say, night after night, until the day-spring of that glory bursts upon you, "I will both lie down and sleep in peace, for You alone, O Lord, make me live in safety!" — Psalm 4:8

17th Evening
THE PROMISES OF GOD

"For all the promises of God in Him are *Yes*, and in Him *Amen*." — 2 Corinthians 1:20

God has made a Will, or Testament, in behalf of His people! It is signed and sealed. It cannot be altered — nothing can divest us of our inheritance. The bequest is His own "exceeding great and precious promises." What a heritage! All that the sinner requires — all that the sinner's God can give. In this testamentary deed there are no *contingencies* — no *perhaps*. The testator commences it with the sure guarantee for its every jot and tittle being fulfilled, "Truly, truly, I say unto you!" He endorses every promise, and every page, with a "Yes, and Amen." "God, willing more abundantly to show to the heirs of promise the immutability of His counsel, confirmed it by an oath."

Who provided such a rich Promise Treasury? What is the *source*, where is the fountain-head, from which these *streams of mercy* flow to the Church? "In HIM." Believer! from Jesus every promise is derived — in Jesus every promise centers. Pardon, peace, adoption, consolation, eternal life — all "in Him." In Him you are "chosen," "called," "justified," "sanctified," and "glorified." You have in possession all the blessings of *present grace;* you have in reserve all the happiness of *coming glory!* And "He who has promised is faithful."

Your *friends* may deceive you — the *world* has deceived you — the Lord never will! Myriads in glory, are there to tell how not one thing has failed of all that the Lord their God has spoken. Rely on this faithfulness. He gave His Son for you. After the greater blessing — surely you may trust Him for subordinate ones. And where do these promises beam most brightly? Like the stars, it is in the *night!* In the midnight of trial — when the sun of earthly prosperity has set — when deep is calling to deep, and wave to wave; when tempted, bereaved, beaten down with "a great fight of afflictions," the spiritual sky with its *galaxy of Promises* is brightest and clearest!

But do not be deceived; the night of sorrow cannot 'in itself' give you the comfort of the Divine Promises. It may be night — and yet the stars invisible. It is only "in Him" these promises can be discerned in their luster. Reader! if you are "outside of Christ," these *stars of Gospel promise* shine in vain to you; they have, to the unspiritual eye, no beauty or brightness. The guiding pillar, so lustrous to the chosen people — was a column of portentous gloom to Pharaoh's army. But "in Him," as "heirs of God," you are inheritors of "all the promises." All the promises! Oh! with such a pillow whereon to rest your aching head, you may well resume your nightly song, "I will both lie down and sleep in peace, for You alone, O Lord, make me live in safety!" — Psalm 4:8

18th Evening
THE WARNINGS OF GOD

"Keeping mercy for thousands, forgiving iniquity and transgression and sin. Yet He does not leave the guilty unpunished." — Exodus 34:7

"He is faithful who *promised*." Do we bear sufficiently in mind another truth of equal fidelity — He is faithful who *threatens?* Ponder that solemn word, "Yet He does not leave the guilty unpunished!" Remember when that word was spoken it was in connection with a sublime apocalypse of God's majesty. It was as "the glory of the Lord" was passing before Moses. Was not this intended to show, that there is a solemn and inseparable connection between the Divine glory — and the impossibility of God's leaving the guilty unpunished? It was at a time, moreover, when the benignity of God was intended to be more specially manifested. It was when He was declared to be "the Lord, the Lord God, merciful, gracious, long-suffering, abundant in goodness." Then it was, we listen to the solemn note of warning, that He will not, and cannot leave the guilty unpunished!

His law requires — the honor of His throne requires; demands that the guilty be punished. Reader! are you still clinging to a dream of final mercy? Do you believe in the first part of the Divine proclamation at Sinai, and persist in presumptuous and fatal skepticism with regard to the last? That boundless in His resources, and infinite in His love, God will, by some means, "leave the guilty unpunished?" Do not be deceived, that you do not incur the woe of him who "strives with his Maker." The Lord, who "is not slack concerning His *promises*," cannot be slack concerning His *threatenings*.

Time blunts the wrath of *man*; and softens and subdues the turbulence of his passions; but there is no blind impulse — no vacillation in Him with whom "a thousand years are as one day." "God's threatenings," says a writer, "are God's doings!" The Law has not one breathing of mercy for you. There is not one cleft in all Mount Sinai where you can escape the vengeance of the storm. Unless you flee without delay to Him who has "cleared the guilty" by Himself — the Guiltless One, becoming the guilt-bearer; be assured that through eternity, you will surely be punished.

My soul! are you yet in this state of perilous estrangement from God? You are still launched on the cheerless ocean of uncertainty; leaving everything to a dying hour; the time to which nothing should be left — but to die! Ponder these living words of unchanging truth, "Though hand join in hand, the wicked shall not escape unpunished!" The *golden chain of grace* stretches from Heaven to earth — but it can go no further, "Seek the Lord *while* He may be found." There is solemn warning in that one word. It tells you, there is a day coming, when the Lord will be sought — but will not be found.

Reader! cast yourself this night at His footstool; implore His mercy. Rise not from your bended knees, until, with His propitiated smile gladdening you, and the hope of His Heaven cheering you — you may (it may be for the first time in your life) lie down with a quiet conscience and a pardoned soul on your nightly couch, exclaiming, "I will both lie down and sleep in peace, for You alone, O Lord, make me live in safety!" — Psalm 4:8

19th Evening
THE CHASTISEMENTS OF GOD

"For whom the Lord loves — He chastens; and scourges every son whom He receives." — Hebrews 12:6

Chastisement is the family badge — the family pledge — the family privilege, "To you it is *granted* to suffer." "Troubles," says a godly man, "are in God's catalogue of mercies." "Afflictions," says another, "are God's hired laborers to break the clods and plow the land." Reader, is the hand of your God heavy upon you? Has He been breaking your *cisterns*, withering your *gourds*, poisoning your sweetest *fountains* of earthly bliss? Are the world's bright spots outnumbered by the dreary ones? Has one tear been following another in quick succession? You may have to tell, perhaps, of a varied experience of trials. Every tender point touched — sickness, bereavement, poverty — perhaps all of these.

Be still. If you are a child of God, there is *no exemption* from the "household discipline." The rod is the Father's; the *voice* that speaks may be rough — but the *hand* that smites is gentle. The *furnace* may be seven times heated — but the *Refiner* is seated nearby. His object is not to consume — but to *purify*. Do not misinterpret His dealings; there is mercy on the wings of "the rough wind." Our choicest fountains are fed from dark lowering clouds. All, be assured, will yet bear the stamp of divine love. *Sense* cannot yet discern "the *rainbow* in the clouds." Aged Jacob exclaimed at first, "All these things are against me!" but at last he had a calmer and a more just verdict, and "his spirit revived!"

"At evening time it was light." The saint on *earth* can say, regarding his trials, in faith and in trust, "I *know*, O Lord, that Your judgments are right." The saint in *glory* can go a step farther, "I *see*, O Lord, that they are so!" His *losses* will then be shown to be his *riches*. Believer! on a calm retrospect of your heaviest afflictions — say, were they unneeded? This "severe mercy of God's discipline" — was it too severe? *Less* would not have done. Like Jonah, you never would have awoke — but for the *storm*. He may have led you to a Zarephath (a place of furnaces) — but it is to show you "one like unto the Son of God!" When was God ever so near to you, or you to your God — as in the furnace-fires?

When was the *presence* and *love* and *sympathy* of Jesus so precious? It was when "the Beloved" comes down from the *Mountain of Myrrh* and the *Hill of Frankincense* — to His Garden on earth. He can get no fragrance from some plants but by *bruising* them. The spices in the Temple of old were *crushed*. The gold of its candlestick was *beaten* gold! It was when the Marah-fountain of your heart was bitter with sin — that He cast in some cross, some trial, and "the waters were made sweet!"

My soul, be still! You have, in affliction, one means of glorifying God, which even angels have not, in their sorrowless world — patience under the rod — submission to your Heavenly Father's will! Pray not to have your affliction *removed* — but for grace to *bear up* under it, so that you may glorify God even "in the fires!" Remember that though "weeping endures for a night — joy comes in the morning!" Close your tearful eyes, saying, "I will both lie down and sleep in peace, for You alone, O Lord, make me live in safety!" — Psalm 4:8

20th Evening
THE INVITATIONS OF GOD

"All whom the Father gives Me — will come to Me; and whoever comes to Me — I will never cast out." — John 6:37

How *broad* is the door of welcome! Before the prodigal son, the ungrateful returning wanderer, could stammer forth through penitential tears the confession of his sins — the arms of his father's mercy were around him! The prodigal son thought of no more than the servant's place; the father had in readiness the best robe and the fattened calf! God has the first word in the overtures of mercy. He refuses none — He welcomes all — the poor — the wretched — the blind — the naked — the burdened — the heavy laden — the hardened sinner — the aged sinner — the daring sinner — the dying sinner — ALL are invited to come! *"Come now, let us reason together!* says the Lord. *Though your sins are like scarlet — they shall be as white as snow; though they are red as crimson — they shall be like wool!"*

The most parched tongue that laps the streams from the smitten Rock — has everlasting life! "When *we* forgive — it costs us an effort; when *God* forgives — it is His delight." From the battlements of Heaven He is calling after us: "Turn, turn! Why will you die?" He seems to wonder if sinners have pleasure in their own death. He declares, "I have no pleasure in the death of the wicked; but that the wicked turn from his way and live!"

Reader! have you yet closed with the Gospel's free invitation? Have you gone to Him, just as you are — with all the raggedness of nature's garments — standing in your own nothingness — feeling that you are insolvent — that, you have "nothing to pay," already a bankrupt, and the debt always increasing? Have you taken hold of that blessed assurance, "He is able to save to the uttermost"? Are you resting your *eternal all* on Him who has done all and suffered all, for you; leaving you, "without money and without price," a free, full, unconditional offer of a great salvation?

Do not say that your sins are too *many* — the crimson dye too *deep*. It is because you are a great *sinner*, and have great *sins* — that you need a great *Savior!* "Of whom I am the chief," is a *golden postscript* to "the faithful saying — that Jesus came into the world to save sinners." Do not dishonor God by casting doubts on His willingness or ability. If your sins are heinous, you will be all the more an amazing monument of grace! You may be the weakest and unworthiest of vessels; but, remember, there was a *niche* in the Temple for both the *great* and for the *small* — for the cups, as well as for the pitchers. Even the smallest vessel glorifies Christ.

Arise then, call upon the Lord! We cannot say, with the king of Nineveh, "Who can tell? God may yet relent and with compassion *turn* from His fierce anger so that we will not perish!" He is turning now — declaring, on His own immutable Word, that "whoever comes to Me — I will never cast out." "Though you have lived among the pots — you shall be as the wings of a dove, covered with silver, and her feathers with yellow gold!" Close, without delay, with these precious invitations, that so, looking up to a reconciled God and Father in Heaven, you may even this night say, "I will both lie down and sleep in peace, for You alone, O Lord, make me live in safety!" — Psalm 4:8

21st Evening
THE CONSOLATIONS OF GOD

"Comfort, comfort My people, says your God." — Isaiah 40:1

God's people are prone to be discouraged because of the *difficulty* of the way. In the bitterness of their spirits, they are often apt to say, with desponding Zion, "The Lord has forsaken me!" Or with the faithless prophet, "It is better for me to die than to live!"

But the Christian has his consolations too, and they are "strong consolations." The "still small voice" mingles with the hurricane and the storm. The bush burns with fire — but the great God is in the bush, and therefore it is indestructible! "The Lord lives, and blessed be my rock; and may the God of my salvation be exalted!" Earthly consolations may help to dry one tear — but another tear is ready to flow. God dries *all* tears. There is no need in the aching voids of the heart — which He cannot supply.

Is it *mercy to pardon?* I can look up to the throne of the Most High God — and see Holiness and Righteousness, Justice and Truth, all bending, in exulting harmony, over my ruined soul, exclaiming, "This is a faithful saying, and worthy of all acceptance, that Jesus Christ came into the world to save sinners!" Is it *grace to help?* I can look up to that same throne, and behold, seated thereon, a Great High Priest — no, a mighty Prince, having power with God, and prevailing — prayer without ceasing ascending from His lips in behalf of His people!

When *Satan* seeks "to sift" them — His upholding power protects them. When *temptation* assails them in their earthly conflicts — the *true Moses* on the Mount, with hands that never "grow heavy," makes them "more than conquerors!" When *trial* threatens to prostrate them, He identifies Himself with the sufferers — He points to His own sorrows, to show them how light the heaviest of earth's sorrows are. Even over the gloomy portals of the *grave* He can write, "Blessed are the dead who die in the Lord!" He alone felt Death's *substance.* His people only see "the *shadow.*" He makes it a Valley of Achor, through which "the two spies," *Faith* and *Hope,* fetch back Eshcol-pledges of the true Land of Promise!

Reader, are you now weary or desponding? Is some *cross* heavy on you — some *trial* oppressing you — some *thorn* in the flesh sorely lacerating you? Be still! He will make His grace sufficient. If He has *allured you into the wilderness* — it is that He may speak comfortably to you. He has an *antidote* for every sorrowful bosom — a *balm* for every wound — a *comfort* for every pang — a *solace* for every tear. "When anxiety was great within me — Your consolation brought joy to my soul." "I will both lie down and sleep in peace, for You alone, O Lord, make me live in safety!" — Psalm 4:8

22nd Evening
THE PATHS OF GOD

"All the *paths* of the LORD are mercy and truth — unto such as keep His covenant and His testimonies." — Psalm 25:10

"All the paths." It is no small effort of faith to say so, when *blessings* are blighted, and *schemes* crossed, and fellow-pilgrims, (it may be beloved spouses in our spiritual joys) are mysteriously removed, to say, "All — ALL is mercy! All — ALL is well!" They are "the paths of the Lord" — His choosing; and, be assured, He will "lead His people by a *right* way." It may not be the way of *their* own selecting. It may be the very last path *they* would have chosen. But when He leads His sheep, "He goes before them." The Shepherd portions off our pasture-ground. He guides the *footsteps* of the flock. He will lead them by no rougher way — than He sees needful. Does a human father give his child his own way? If he did — it would be his ruin! Will God surrender us to our own truant wills — which are often bent on wandering farthest from Him? No! He knows us better! He loves us better!

Believer, it is the loftiest triumph and prerogative of faith, to have no *way* — no *path* of your own — but with childlike simplicity and reliance to say, "Teach me Your paths. Lead me *however* and *wherever* You please. Let it be through the darkest, loneliest, thorniest way — only let it bring me nearer Yourself!"

Would that we could keep our eye not so much on the *path* — as on the *bright gate*, which terminates it. When standing at that luminous portal, we shall trace, with adoring wonder, the way in which our God has led us; discerning the "need be" of every teardrop! And to the question, *"Is it well?"* to which often on earth we gave an evasive answer — we will be ready with an unhesitating reply, *"It is well!"* What a *light* will then be flashed on these three often mysterious words, *"God is love!"* Then, at last, shall we be able to add the joyful comment, "We have known and believed the love which God has to us!"

Meanwhile, Reader! if you are treading a path of sorrow, consider, as an encouragement, that your Lord and Master trod the same before you. Behold, as He toiled on *His blood-stained journey*, how *submission to the Divine will* formed the secret of His support. "Yes,

Father, because this was Your good pleasure!" "Not My will — but may Your will be done!" The *True David* was strengthened with what sustained His typical ancestor in a dark and trying hour: "O Lord, You are my God!"

Believer, if it is your God in covenant who is leading you — then what more can you require? "His Ways are truth and judgment." He will guide you by His counsel, while you live — and afterward receive you into glory! My God! if such is the design of Your dealings and discipline, "I will both lie down and sleep in peace, for You alone, O Lord, make me live in safety!" — Psalm 4:8

23rd Evening
THE SECRET OF GOD

"The secret of the LORD is with those who fear him; and He will show them His covenant." — Psalm 25:14

Believer, your God has some mighty secret to confide to you! What is this, which (a mystery to the world), is to be conveyed in whispers into the ears of His people! "He will show them His Covenant!" Listen, this night, to this blessed "secret." You have pondered it often before. But its wonders never diminish by repetition.

The *Author* of it is God — the Eternal Father. He framed its articles before the foundation of the world. It wrong to represent the *atonement* as the *cause* of God's love. God's love was rather the originating cause of the atonement. "God so *loved* the world — that He *gave* His one and only Son." How runs the Covenant-Charter? "Everything belongs to you .... the whole world and life and death; the present and the future. Everything belongs to you, and you belong to Christ, and Christ belongs to God."

The initiative — the first overture of covenant-mercy, was with Him. It was the *insulted Sovereign* who first dreamed of mercy towards the rebels! It was the *injured Father* who first thought of His ungrateful children. Wondrous secret — that from all eternity, the Heart of God was *all LOVE* to us!

Think of the *Surety* of the Covenant. It was the adorable Son of the Father. He voluntarily accepted the Covenant stipulations: "Lo, I come! I delight to do Your will, O My God!" He ceased not, until, all the terms being fulfilled, He could claim His stipulated reward: "I have glorified You on the earth, I have finished the work which You gave Me to do." And still He lives, and reigns, and intercedes, under the blessed title of *"Mediator of the Everlasting Covenant!"*

Think of the Almighty *Dispenser* of the blessings of the Covenant. It is the *Spirit* of all Grace — the third person in the ever-blessed, co-equal Trinity.

Think of the *Heirs* of the Covenant. They are all who, by simple faith, are willing to appropriate its inestimable blessings.

Think of the *Security* of the Covenant. There is much *uncertainty* in all earthly agreements. But all is certainty in the Covenant, *"I will be your God — and you shall My people."* This unfailing Covenant has the rock of Christ's Deity to rest upon; and a Triune God pledged to make good all its provisions, "My covenant I will not break — nor alter the Word that has gone out of My mouth!"

Think of the *Perpetuity* of the Covenant: "I will betroth you unto Me *forever!*"

Think of the rich *Inheritance* of the Covenant. Oh! here is the mighty secret of unfathomable love: "If we are His children, then Heirs — Heirs of God." "Heirs of God!" Our in hesitance is all within the scope of Omnipotence to bestow! He puts His hand to a *blank check*, that His people may write under it whatever they please, which is for their good.

My soul! are you an heir of God? Can you look upwards to the throne of that "Great I am," and say, "This God is my God!" Happier words — a more glorious assurance — cannot thrill on an archangel's tongue! With such a *Portion* as this — surely I need no other! Let that amazing "secret" form the last thought of this day; and, as the Almighty is even now whispering it in my ears, I may close my eyes, repeating, "I will both lie down and sleep in peace, for You alone, O Lord, make me live in safety!" — Psalm 4:8

24th Evening
THE NAME OF GOD

"The *name* of the Lord is a strong tower! The righteous run into it — and are safe." — Proverbs 18:10

Strong indeed! "We have a strong city; God makes salvation its walls and ramparts." Every ATTRIBUTE of the Godhead is such a tower. Every *perfection* such a rampart — all combined to insure the believer's everlasting security! Reader, "Go, inspect the city of Jerusalem.

Walk around and count the many towers. Take note of the fortified walls, and tour all the citadels, that you may describe them to future generations. For that is what God is like. He is our God forever and ever, and He will be our guide until we die!"

Mark the strong Tower of divine OMNIPOTENCE. It proclaims that the Almighty God is on your side — that there is One with you and for you, boundless in His resources, greater far than all that can be against you!

Mark the strong Tower of divine UNCHANGEABLENESS. All *earthly* fabrics are tottering and crumbling around you. The dearest of all your earthly refuges has written on it — the doom of the dust! But, sheltered here, you can gaze on all the fitful changes of life, and exult in an unchanging God!

Mark the strong Tower of divine WISDOM. When His dealings are dark, and chastisements mysterious, you must retire within this fortress — and to be reminded that all, all that befalls you, is the planning of unerring rectitude and faithfulness! See inscribed on the chamber-walls, "The only Wise God!"

Mark the strong Tower of divine LOVE. When the *hurricane* has been fierce, your heart breaking with new trials, the past dark, the future a dreary waste, no *lull* in the storm, no *light* in the clouds — oh! It is a great comfort to you to retire into this most hallowed of bulwarks, and read the living motto emblazoned on its every turret, *"God is love!"*

My soul! are you safe in this impregnable fortress? Have you entered within the gate? Remember, it is not to be "near" the city — but "in" it. Not to know *about* Christ — but to "win Him, and be found in Him." One footstep outside the walls, and the *Avenger of blood* can cut you down! "Turn, then, to the stronghold!" as a "prisoner of hope!"

Once, these were colossal walls to 'exclude'. Now, they are unassailable barriers to 'protect'! They are now a *citadel* where His saints are "kept" by the power of God. Every portal is open; and the God of Mercy issues the gracious proclamation, "Come, My people, enter into your chambers!" How safe! how happy here!

IN GOD! "There is, in this," says Jonathan Edwards, speaking of the same blessed truth, "secured to me, as it were — a calm, sweet aspect, or appearance, of glory in almost everything." We can hear, amid the surges of life, a voice high above the storm, the Name of the Lord, "It is I! Do not be afraid!"

"It is I," remarks Newman Hall, "were as much as a hundred names. It is I — your Lord and Master! It is I — the Commander of winds and waters! It is I — the Sovereign Lord of Heaven and Earth! Let Heaven be but as one Scroll, and let it be written all over with titles — they cannot express more than — *It is I!* Oh, sweet and seasonable word of a gracious Savior! — able to calm all tempests — able to revive all hearts — say but so to my soul, and I am safe!" "I will both lie down and sleep in peace, for You alone, O Lord, make me live in safety!" — Psalm 4:8

25th Evening
THE FAVOR OF GOD

"In His favor is life!" — Psalm 30:5

How anxious are we to stand well with our fellow-men, and secure their favor! Are we equally so to stand well with God? The favor of *man* — what is it? A passing breath, which a *moment* may alienate, a *look* forfeit, and which, at best, a few brief years will forever terminate! But the favor of *God* — how ennobling, constant, and enduring! In possession of His favor, we are independent alike of what the world either gives — or withholds. With it, we are rich — whatever else we lack! Without it, we are poor — though we have the wealth of worlds beside! Bereft of Him, we can truly say with aged Jacob, "I am bereaved!" *Nothing can compensate for His loss — but He can compensate for the loss of everything!*

Reader! are you a stranger to His favor, under the cheerless sense of alienation from God? Sin un-cancelled; peace un-purchased; all uncertainty about the question of your eternity? Who need ask, living thus, if you are satisfied, or happy? *Satisfied?* Impossible! Nothing can satisfy your infinite capacities — but the infinite God. Nothing can fill up the aching voids of your immortal being — but Him "who only has immortality." *Happy?* Impossible! There can be no happiness with sin unforgivin; the conscience unappeased; eternal interests hanging overhead unsettled and unadjusted; death, and judgment, and eternity, all un-provided for! Living at this "dying rate," peace must be a stranger to your bosom!

Seek to make up your peace with God. Covet His life-giving favor. What a *blessed fountain of unsullied joy* has that soul which can look up to Heaven and say, "God is mine!" That word — that thought — wipes away every tear-drop — *"My Father!"* What though the perishable streams are dried, if you are driven to learn the truth, "All my springs are in You!" He may empty your *cistern* — but the *Fountainhead* remains. Job was the sorest of sufferers — but he could bear patiently to be bereft of all, save One, "Oh that I knew where I might find *Him!*"

"Go," said Chrysostom, exulting in this favor of the King of kings, when an earthly princess tried to shake his spirit, *"Go, tell her that I fear nothing but sin!"* Blessed state of conscious security!

The same mighty consolation which supported Jesus in His season of humiliation, forms the solace and rejoicing of His true people, "Because He is on my right hand — I shall not be moved." Blessed Jesus! Oh encompass me this night with Your favor as with a shield, and then, "I will both lie down and sleep in peace, for You alone, O Lord, make me live in safety!" — Psalm 4:8

26th Evening
THE JEWELS OF GOD

"And they shall be Mine, says the LORD Almighty, in that day when I make up *My jewels.*" — Malachi 3:17

"MY JEWELS!" (or, My special treasure!) Of what favored creatures does Jehovah thus speak? Is it of seraphs? Is it of angels? Methinks, at such a title, even they would take the dust of abasement, and veiling their faces, cry, "Unclean! unclean!" But, marvel of marvels! It is *redeemed sinners* of the earth — once crude, unshapely stones, lying in "the horrible pit and the miry clay," amid the rubbish of corruption — who are thus sought out by divine grace, purchased by divine love, destined through eternity to be set as jewels in the crown of the eternal God!

"The Lord's *portion* is His people!" There is a surpassing revelation of love here. Great, unspeakably great, is the privilege of the believer, to be able to look up to the everlasting Jehovah, and say, "You are my portion, O Lord!" But what is this in comparison with the response of Omnipotence to the child of dust, "You are Mine!" Reader, have you learned to lisp your part in this wondrous interchange of covenant-love, "My beloved is Mine — and I am His!"

What an array of wondrous titles belong to the saints of God, and given, too, by God Himself, in His own Word! He calls them — Sons! Brethren! Princes! Friends! Heirs! Jewels! My Portion! Mine!

And *when* is the time when they become thus dear to Him? Sinner, when you wept at the cross of Jesus, and joined yourself in covenant with God — you became His jewel. No — from eternity past — "He has loved you with an *everlasting* love!" True, you are not yet set in His *crown.* You are yet undergoing the process of *polishing.* Affliction is preparing you; trial is needed to remove all the roughness and blemishes of nature, and make you *fit* for your Master's use. But, blessed thought! "Now it is God who has made us (literally, *chiseled* or *polished* us) for this very purpose and has given us the Spirit as a deposit, guaranteeing what is to come." Yes, God Himself, the possessor, who prized that earthly jewel so much, as to give in exchange for it Heaven's "Pearl of great price!" He has the *polishing* in His own hand! He will not deal too rashly or roughly.

And where, meanwhile, is the *casket* in which these jewels are kept until the coronation-day arrives, when the crown of His Church triumphant (every saint a gem) will be placed on the head of Jesus? It is He, their Purchaser, their Proprietor, who preserves them. They are "kept by the power of God." Our great High Priest, the *true Aaron*, has them set in His breastplate; He bears them on His *heart* on His every approach to the throne. They are the precious stones set in gold upon the ephod! And though the *sins* of His people, and the schemes of Satan, combine in doing what they can to destroy them, He declares that none shall ever pluck them out of His hand, or from His heart!

A jewel in Immanuel's crown! Not only raised from the ash-heap to be set among princes, but to gem through eternity — the Forehead that for me, was once wreathed with thorns!

Shall I — can I — murmur at any way my Savior sees fit to *polish* and *prepare* me for such an honor as this? Let me sink down on my nightly pillow overpowered with the thought; and as I hear my covenant God whispering in my ear the astounding accents, "You are Mine!" I may well reply, "I will both lie down and sleep in peace, for You alone, O Lord, make me live in safety!" — Psalm 4:8

27th Evening
THE JUDGMENT OF GOD

"For we must all appear before the judgment seat of Christ, that each one may receive what is due him for the things done while in the body — whether good or bad." — 2 Corinthians 5:10

ALL must appear! There is no eluding His searching scrutiny! Believer, there is to you no terror in that coming reckoning. The judicial dealing between yourself and your God is already past. You are already acquitted. The moment you cast yourself at the cross of your dear Lord, the sentence of "Not Guilty!" was pronounced upon you; and if "it is God who justifies — then who can condemn?" But this sentence will be ratified and openly proclaimed before an assembled world. On that *great day of disclosures* God will avenge His own elect. All the calumnies and aspersions heaped on their character will be wiped away. In the presence of devils, and angels, and men — the approving sentence will go forth from the lips of the Omniscient One, "Enter into the joy of your Lord!"

And WHO is to be your Judge? Who is to be enthroned on that tribunal of unerring rectitude, before whom every knee is to bow and every heart is to be laid open? "For He has set a day when He will judge the world with justice by THAT MAN He has appointed." "That Man!" Oh, it is no stranger! It is Him who died for you! who is now interceding for you! who will then stand to espouse your cause, vindicate your integrity, and utter the challenge to every reclaiming adversary, "Who shall lay anything to the charge of God's elect?"

Reader, seek to know this *God-Man Mediator* on a throne of *grace,* before you meet Him on a throne of *judgment!* Seek to have your name now enrolled in this Book of Life, that you may hear it then confessed before His "Father and the holy angels." What an incentive to increased aspirations after holiness and higher spiritual attainments, to remember that the awards of that day and of eternity — will be determined by the transactions of time! It is a grand Bible principle, that though *justified* by faith — we shall be *judged* by works. No more, while from first to last, Jesus, and Jesus alone, is the *meritorious* cause of salvation — yet the works flowing from faith in Him and love to Him, will regulate the degree of future bliss; whether we shall be among the "greatest" or "the least in the kingdom;" whether we shall occupy the outskirts of glory, or revolve in orbits around the throne in the blaze of God's immediate presence!

Were that trumpet-blast now to break on your ear, would you be prepared with the welcome response, "Even so, come Lord Jesus!" Seek to be living in this habitual state of holy preparedness, that even the midnight cry would not take you by surprise; that the summons which will prove so startling to a slumbering world, would be to you the herald of glory, "He comes, He comes to judge the earth!"

Oh the blessedness of being able, in sweet confidence in the Savior's second coming, to compose myself to rest night after night, and say, "Even though the trumpet of judgment should break upon my ears, I will both lie down and sleep in peace, for You alone, O Lord, make me live in safety!" — Psalm 4:8

28th Evening
GOD'S BANQUETING HOUSE

"He brought me to the banqueting house, and His banner over me was love!" — Song of Solomon 2:4

"HE brought me!" All of grace! He justifies! He glorifies! The top-stone is brought forth, the banqueting house is entered with shoutings, saying, "Grace, grace unto it!" Believer, contemplate the *journey* ended, the *course* finished, the *victory* won. Seated at the marriage feast of the Lamb in glory, guest talking to guest with bounding hearts — recounting their Lord's dealings on earth — the watchword circulating from tongue to tongue, *"He has done all things well!"*

Angels and archangels, too, will be participants in that banquet of glory; and bright seraphs, who never knew what it was to have a heart of sin or to shed a tear of sorrow. But, for this reason, there will be one element of joy peculiar to the Redeemed, into which the other unfallen guests cannot enter — the "joy of contrast." How will this present world's "great tribulation" augment the bliss of a world at once sinless and sorrowless! How will earth's woe-worn cheek, and sin-stricken spirit, and tear-dimmed eye — enhance the glories of that perfect state, where there is not that symbol of sadness, nor the solitary trace of one lingering tear-drop!

Then will be realized that *sweet paradox:* "They rest" — "They rest not!" "The rest without a rest." "They rest" — the eternal pause and cessation from all the feverish disquietudes of this world's sins and sorrows; all that would disturb the rapture of a holy repose. And yet, it is but the *restless activity of holiness* — the Divine energy of beings whose grand element of happiness is employment in the service and executing of the will of God. In this "they cease not day nor night."

It is sublimely said of the God before whom they hymn their anthems and cast their crowns, that *"He inhabits the praises of eternity!"* My soul, seek often to ponder, in the midst of your days of sadness, the joys of that eternal banqueting house. "He will wipe every tear from their eyes. There will be no more death or mourning or crying or pain!" One *moment* at that banquet table — one *crumb* of the heavenly manna — one *draught* from the river of life

— and all the bitter experiences of the valley of tears will be obliterated and forgotten!

Look upwards even now, and behold your dear Lord preparing for you this glorious "feast of fat things!" "Do not be troubled. There are many rooms in My Father's home, and I am going to prepare a place for you. When everything is ready, I will come and get you, so that you will always be with Me where I am!" He has Himself entered the banqueting house as the pledge and forerunner of the coming guests. He, the first Sheaf of the mighty harvest, has been waved before God in the temple of the New Jerusalem, as a pledge of the immortal sheaves still to be gathered into the heavenly garner!

The invitation is issued, "Come, for all things are ready!" "The feast has been prepared, and choice meats have been cooked. Everything is ready. Hurry to the wedding banquet!" Reader, prepare for the feast — suitably attire yourself for such a glorious banquet. Put on your beautiful garments — that righteousness of Jesus, without which you cannot be accepted — that holiness of heart, without which no one can see the Lord. Soon shall *the little hour of life's unquiet dream* be over; and then, oh the glorious surprise of being ushered into that banqueting table — to know, forever — the blessedness of those "who are called unto the marriage-supper of the Lamb!"

With the prospect of such joys awaiting me in the *morning of immortality*, with the dark nights of death before me, and the grave my couch, I shall be able to say, even of its lonely chamber, "I will both lie down and sleep in peace, for You alone, O Lord, make me live in safety!" — Psalm 4:8

29th Evening
THE PRESENCE OF GOD

"In Your presence is fullness of joy!" — Psalm 16:11

Even in this world, where the Christian can only dimly apprehended God — how sweet is the sense of His presence, and friendship, and love! What will it be in that eternal world — where He is seen in *open vision!* If the *foretaste* is blessed — what must be the *fruition!* If the *rays* of the Divine glory are gladdening — what must be the *full blaze* of that Sun itself!

Believer, do you often delight to pause in your journey? Does faith love to ascend its Pisgah Mount and get a prospect of this Land of Promise? What is the grand feature and element which swallows up all the circumstantials in your future bliss? Let Patriarchs, Prophets, and Apostles, answer — It is "Your Presence!" "In my flesh, I shall see God!" says one. "I shall be satisfied," says another, "when I awake, with Your likeness!" "They shall see His face!" says a third. Amid all the glowing visions of a coming Heaven granted to John in Patmos, there *is One all-glorious object* that has ever a peerless and distinctive pre-eminence — God Himself!

There is no *sun* — Why? "For the Lord God gives them light." There is no *temple* — Why? "For the Lord God and the Lamb are the temple thereof." The saints dwell in holy brotherhood; but what is the mighty bond of their union; their chief joy? "He who sits on the Throne shall dwell among them!" They have no longer the intervention of ordinances and means — Why? Because "the Lamb who is in the midst of the Throne shall feed them, and lead them to living fountains of waters." They no longer draw on the storehouse of the *Promises* — Why? Because "God Himself shall wipe away all tears from their eyes." Reader, here is the true "Peniel," where you will *"see God face to face."* Here is the true "Mahanaim," where the Angels of God meet you.

In Heaven is the true communion of *saints* — the glorious fellowship of the *Prophets* — the goodly fellowship of the *Apostles* — the noble army of *Martyrs*. Yet all these will be subservient and subordinate to the first — the vision and fruition of God! Even the recognition of *death-divided* loved ones (that sweet element in the believer's prospect of bliss) will pale, in comparison, before this

"Glory that excels!"

Are you among these "pure in heart," who are to "see God"? Remember the Bible's solemn warning, "Without holiness no man shall see the Lord." Remember its solemn admonition, "And every man who has this hope fixed on Him, *purifies himself* even as He is pure." To "see God!" Oh, what *preparation* is needed for so magnificent a contemplation! *Infinite unworthiness and nothingness*, to stand in the presence of *Infinite Majesty, Purity, and Glory!*

Can I wonder at the *much discipline* required, before I can be thus "presented faultless before the presence of His glory?" How will these needed *furnace-fires* be dimmed into nothing — when viewed from the Sapphire throne! Heart and flesh may be fainting and failing; but, remembering that that same God is now "the strength of my heart," who is to be my "portion forever;" I may joyfully say, "I will both lie down and sleep in peace, for You alone, O Lord, make me live in safety!" — Psalm 4:8

30th Evening
The Path of Duty

"Then the devil took him to the holy city and had him stand on the highest point of the temple. 'If you are the Son of God,' he said, 'throw yourself down. For it is written: He will command his angels concerning you, and they will lift you up in their hands, so that you will not strike your foot against a stone.' Jesus answered him, 'It is also written: You must not tempt the Lord your God!'" Matthew 4:5-7

When one method of temptation fails — then Satan tries another. He has many different arrows in his quiver — as the tempted saints of God know full well! And, in his attacks upon the Son of God, he showed that he was not lacking in varied expedients, if by any means he might gain advantage over him. Having been unsuccessful in attempting to generate a spirit of distrust — he was planning what could be done in connection with the opposite feeling of presumption.

The scene of this temptation was one of the pinnacles of the temple, probably that of Solomon's porch, which overlooked an immense precipice between six and seven hundred feet in depth. Speaking of this prodigious elevation, the Jewish historian says that no one could look down from it without becoming giddy. After having conducted the Savior to this solemn eminence, Satan made the impious proposal that, in order to prove his sonship, he should throw himself from the top to the bottom. "If you are the Son of God — throw yourself down. For it is written: He will command his angels concerning you, and they will lift you up in their hands, so that you will not strike your foot against a stone!"

Inasmuch as our Lord resisted the former proposal by quoting from the sacred writings, the cunning adversary seems to have thought that he could not do better than follow his example. But if we compare the original Old Testament passage — we find a material difference, in consequence of an important omission, one sentence being altogether left out. As recorded in the 91st Psalm, the words are, "If you make the Most High your dwelling — even the Lord, who is my refuge — then no harm will befall you, no disaster will come near your tent. For he will command his angels concerning you to protect you in all your ways!"

God has promised to protect his people — but only while they are walking in his ways. The path of duty — is the path of safety. So, if we rush heedlessly into temptation — we cannot expect to be kept from evil. The inspired text can be thus twisted, and dragged in for a purpose altogether opposed to its express design — a practice in which the emissaries of the wicked one have largely indulged — wresting the scriptures unto their own destruction, as well as to the ruin of others.

But we may ask, Why did not Satan proceed with the quotation? For the next verse is, "You will trample upon lions and cobras; you will crush fierce lions and serpents under your feet!" Ah! he well knew that this would have touched himself, and so he wisely left it alone. It was a promise, however which was strikingly verified on this occasion; for did not Jesus tread triumphantly upon the old lion, and trample the great serpent under his feet!

As on the former occasion, the Savior's reply was pointed and appropriate, and was taken from the divine oracles. "It is also written: You must not tempt the Lord your God." He takes no notice of Satan's garbled quotation — but meets it at once by one that was accurate and honest; teaching us that however our enemies may misquote and misapply the word of God, this is no reason why we should give up appealing to it as our great standard on all occasions.

The confidence of Christ in his Father's protecting care was such, that he felt there was no necessity to put it to such a trial as this temptation implied. Be it yours, O my soul! to aspire after a similar spirit. While others tempt God, let it be your firm resolve to trust him — and then mercy shall compass you about. The promise is, "He shall call upon me, and I will answer him! I will be with him in trouble; I will deliver him, and honor him."

In every evil day, and under all distressing circumstances, would I call upon your blessed name, O Lord. And since you have never said to the seed of Jacob, Seek me in vain — I have abundant grounds for cherishing the sweet and supporting assurance, that you will be to me what you have been to all your people throughout successive generations — even their refuge and strength, and a very present help in every time of need!

31st Evening
GOD'S CLOSING CALL

"Behold, now is the accepted time; behold, now is the day of salvation." — 2 Corinthians 6:2

Reader! How does it stand with you? Is the question of *your soul's salvation* finally and forever settled? Are you at peace with God? Can you say with Paul, in the prospect of death, "I am now ready!" Have you been led to feel the infinite peril of postponement and procrastination, and responded to the appeal, "Behold, Now!" Ah, how many have found, when the imagined hour of deathbed preparation had come — that the *tear of penitence* was too late to be shed, and the *prayer of mercy* too late to be uttered! Let there be plain dealing between your *conscience* and your *God*. Do not try to escape from the pressing urgency of the question. You may dismiss it now — but there is a day coming when you dare not! Let it not merge in vague generalities — let it be realized as matter of personal concern; of infinite importance to yourself, "Am I saved — or am I not saved? Am I prepared — or am I unprepared, to meet Almighty God?"

You may have, perhaps, an honest intent of giving it some *future* deliberation at another and "more convenient season." Do we ever read of Felix's "more convenient season?" It were better not to risk the experiment of a dying hour, for the solution of the problem, *"Is my soul safe for eternity?"* That it is too difficult a matter — a conference about the soul on the brink of eternity! Remember, God's Spirit "will not always strive." All His other attributes are infinite — but His *patience* and *forbearance* have their "bounds and limits."

The *invitation* which is yours today — may be withdrawn tomorrow! The *axe* may be even now laid at the root of the tree, and the *sentence* on the wing, *"Cut it down!"* How awful, that you are *yet* living in this state of estrangement and guilt! What a surrender of present peace! What a forfeiture of eternal joy! Hurry! flee for your life, lest you be consumed! *Your immortality is no trifle!*

"The night is *far* spent!" Who can tell how far? It may be *now* — or *never* with you! Once more you are about to lie down on your nightly pillow. What if your awaking tomorrow were to be "in outer darkness" in the infernal pit! But, take courage, that night is not *too* far spent. Close this last of the "Night Watches," by fleeing, without delay, to Jesus — the Sinner's Savior and the Sinner's Friend. It was on the *last watch of the night*, He came of old to His tempest-tossed disciples. Like them, receive Him now into your soul; and have all your guilty fears calmed by His omnipotent, *"Peace, be still!"*

Are there not *ominous signs* all around, as if the *world's* last and closing "night-watch" has come? The billows are heaving high. We hear the footsteps on the waters. Amid the fitful moanings of the blast, the watchword is heard — of joy to some, of terror to others, "Maranatha! The Lord is coming!"

Reader! are *you* ready? Is the joyous response on your tongue, "Come, Lord Jesus! Come quickly!" If this night were indeed your very last, and the thunders of judgment were to break upon you before daybreak; would you be able, in the assurance of an eternal dawn, to say, "I will both lie down and sleep in peace, for You alone, O Lord, make me live in safety!" — Psalm 4:8

CPSIA information can be obtained
at www.ICGtesting.com
Printed in the USA
BVHW041530090720
583242BV00006B/536